DOUBLE LIFE

Double Life

SHEILA JEAN HOOD

Tyndale House Publishers, Inc.
Wheaton, Illinois

Scripture quotations, unless otherwise noted, are from *The Holy Bible*, New International Version. Copyright © 1973, 1978, 1984 International Bible Society. Used by permission of Zondervan Bible Publishers.

Library of Congress Catalog Card Number 90-72131
ISBN 0-8423-0549-1
© 1991 by Sheila Hood
All rights reserved
Printed in the United States of America
98 97 96 95 94 93 92 91
9 8 7 6 5 4 3 2 1

*This book is dedicated with a deep love
to my daughter, D E B I,
who walked through the valleys with me.
She was to me a vibrant flower in a barren place.*

CONTENTS

Foreword ix
1. The Test 1
2. Looking Back 13
3. Kneeling before the Altar . 29
4. The Strain of Confession . 41
5. Radical Changes 51
6. The Worst Day 59
7. Faltering Steps of Faith . . 69
8. Given the Choice 83
9. Tearing Inequities 93
10. The "Really" Reason . . . 101
11. Healing 109
12. My Love Journal 115
13. First Reunion 131
14. Debi, Your Dad Has AIDS! 137
15. Living in the
    Knowledge of Death . . . 147
16. A New Grief 157
17. Lingering Pain 163
18. Past Losses, Future Hope 167
19. Clinging to Life 177
20. Hard Pressed,
    But Not Crushed 185
21. On the Twelfth
    Day of June 189
22. Victory Parade 199
23. A New Chapter 211
Epilogue 215

FOREWORD

Although Sheila Hood's story involves the trauma of dealing with the prolonged illness and death of a loved one from Acquired Immune Deficiency Syndrome, this is *not* primarily a book about AIDS.

Although her story involves the tragic impact of sexual addiction and homosexuality, this is *not* a book about homosexuality.

This *is* a book about the hope, help, and healing God offers Christians who suffer the pain inflicted by the sins of others—whatever those sins may be.

Early in my relationship with Sheila and her husband, Bill, she asked, "Is there a hierarchy of sins? Does God hate one sin more than another?" As I told her then, *not as far as I can determine from Scripture!* God includes homosexuality and gossip in the same list of unacceptable behaviors (see 1 Cor. 6:9-10).

Clearly, all sins are equally abhorrent to Him.

Does God hate homosexuals? Absolutely not. He hates what they do with His precious gift of sexuality, but He loves all sinners.

Unfortunately, not all of His professed followers are willing or able to make the same distinction between the sin and the sinner. Some Christians are satisfied to avoid "those kind" of people. It is easy to condemn and withdraw from people who practice the sins we don't. And it is just as easy to tolerate in others the sins we justify in ourselves—the more socially acceptable sins of bitterness, anger, slander, or malice.

Can the Church help homosexuals and those whose lives they touch? What *will* we do with the thousands, perhaps millions of our neighbors who will contract AIDS and die in the next decade? Sheila doesn't have the answers to these questions, but she personalizes the questions for us.

At a San Francisco seminar presented by Exodus International, a national ministry of support to Christians who want to leave the practice of homosexuality, I was one of only two pastors in attendance. Participants made it clear that many of America's fundamentalists or evangelicals have no interest in their work. It was there I heard this tragic indictment: "There are many people in America who believe that homosexuals *cannot* change. Unfortunately, they include not only militant homosexuals but also some Bible-believing Christians."

How sad! Can it be that we who profess to believe in the omnipotent God, who say we believe that the "same power that raised up Jesus" indwells our mortal bodies by His Spirit, believe that God can deliver a person from any sin *except* homosexuality? Can it be that we don't think God would have us love and help those whose lives are threatened by AIDS?

In this book, Sheila Hood tells of her discovery of timeless principles—principles that *work* in the nineties. God's power and presence *are* there for the hopeless and the helpless . . . and the healing support of God's people can *be* there for those who are isolated by fear and failure or feel rejected because of prejudice.

A former practicing homosexual put faith into perspective for all sinners when he said, "I came to the winning side of the battle with my sin when I realized that the center of my faith was not that God *could* deliver me from the practice of my sin, but that God *had* delivered me." The price was paid at the cross, and the power was delivered at Pentecost. Faith simply means that I must *act* on what I believe. Genuine faith is not simply a *statement* of faith; it is daily *acts* of faith. And that's true if it means saying no to a particular sin in my life, or saying yes to the comforting, empowering presence of God that enables me to go on when life is smothering me with intolerance or injustice.

As you read this book, listen for the whisper from a loving heavenly Father: "I will love you when others don't. I will never leave you when others do. I will always provide for you when others won't."

And listen for the heart cries of this dear Christian woman whose agony went largely unnoticed by the Church. Realize that all around us, possibly in our pew on Sunday, are those whose weeping is as private and lonely as Sheila's was. Is there someone to whom you can offer a listening ear? A loving touch? A helping hand? Friendship?

"He who is wise learns from his own experience—he who is wiser from the experience of others." Learn from someone who has been where none of us wants to go—but where many of us could find ourselves in the days ahead!

—Reverend Neal R. Doty, senior pastor
Fairmede Alliance Church, Richmond, California

ACKNOWLEDGMENTS

Thank you, Neal and Jean Doty, Nita Luttrell, Dan Berrner, Michael Donohue, and Sherron Millen. Because you believed in me, I was prompted to begin to write.

Thank you, daughter Debi, Claudia Jarvis, Joe Linn, and Jean and Sean Doty because you kept me from quitting when the hurdles wore me down.

Thank you, Grandma Doty, Pastor Sherman and Ruth Williams, Jr., Pastor Sherm and Marti Williams, III, because your undergirding prayers protected my heart and enabled my mind.

Thank you, Pastor Neal Doty because your wise counsel and masterful way with words have added so much to this book.

Thank you, Dr. Wendell Hawley, Ken Petersen, and Dawn Sundquist because you were so very kind throughout the editorial process.

And a very special thank you to Kin Millen, neighbor and friend. You so generously gave me the gifts of your precious time and your considerable editorial skills when everything that pertained to writing was still foreign to me.

And to the many who have encouraged me along the way: Thank you.

THE TEST *One*

For two weeks now this Thursday had been circled on the calendar. My awareness of the grandfather clock as it methodically announced the passing of the night, its echoes resounding throughout the empty rooms of the house, gave proof I had fooled myself to think that sleep would come in anything more than fitful snatches. As light reentered the room, giving identities to darkened shapes, the shrill buzzing of the alarm clock said it was time to face the day. Wishing this could be just another Thursday, filled with pleasant and familiar routines, could not make it so.

Reluctantly, soberly, I rose from the comfort zone of my bed to prepare for a ten o'clock appointment at the county health office in the nearby suburb of Fremont. The house felt emptier than usual and silent, except for the monologue droning in my head. Even though it resulted in a feeling of loneliness, I was glad that Debi was away at college and unaware of my dilemma. Her own trauma was enough to bear without having to worry about her mother as well.

I approached each task of the morning with calculated consideration. Driving away from the San Francisco commuter traffic by way of the boulevard instead of the freeway, allowing ninety minutes for a forty-minute drive, going alone—all served as a means of following through with the doctor's advice to go in for the test.

I walked out to the car with methodical steps. My thoughts were darting from one scenario to another of what I might later encounter. So absorbed, I proceeded through our quiet little community, beyond the congested streets of the neighboring city, out to the open road and the rolling East Bay hills. By now the sun had risen into the bluest of skies which were softened here and there by billows of white clouds. Hills so recently parched had responded to December rain and were now a deep green in contrast to their earlier days. My unnerving apprehension of the future gradually yielded to the strength of these visual images, which spread like a soothing poultice across my inflamed mind.

The Department of Public Health was strategically located in the center of the city, and as I turned into the parking lot I was relieved to have found my way so easily. It surprised me that no one was visible; I'd envisioned long lines of anonymous people spilling out of the building onto the city sidewalks. The thought of joining the crowd had sent recurring sensations of fear surging from my head to my heart and the pit of my stomach. Now that the fear subsided, humiliation slipped into its place.

As I walked toward the double glass doors of this unfamiliar place, an uncontrollable tear pushed its way past my lashes and was lost in the grey of the concrete stairs. Once inside I stood momentarily to evaluate the facilities—and my courage—as the door closed firmly behind me. Someone had dutifully polished the white-tiled floor. A nondescript bench sat squarely against a pictureless wall. Dull-green heartless arrows pointed the way to the interior of the building. I nervously proceeded down the hall alone. Everything felt functional and cold—hardly conducive to the discussion of gravely intimate concerns.

More signs and arrows led me to a small waiting room, which in contrast to my expectation was empty except for two people. To my right, a woman busily moved about behind a counter that extended from one end of the room to the other. She wore a white uniform, giving her a professional appearance. Directly across from the door and only a few feet away, an intensely thin man sat in the otherwise empty row of orange plastic chairs. My heart sank as my eyes focused on him, his appearance shocking me into the reality of why I had come here on this Thursday morning. I quickly turned toward the woman at the counter.

After a brief explanation, our words were reduced to a minimum as the receptionist passed forms back and forth to me. She appeared unsettled and dropped things repeatedly. Her attempt to explain the procedures that ensured the anonymity of patients sounded impersonal and rehearsed. I responded to her with a smile that belied my inner turmoil. She responded politely with an apologetic look and instructed me to be seated.

I selected the orange chair closest to the door and sat down to apprehensively wait for my turn. Again I was acutely aware of the thin man who sat without motion staring at the floor. If the ruddy color of good health had ever been in his face, it was not there now. His sickly grey skin clung tightly against his protruding bones. Ill-fitting clothes drooped from his frame as though they belonged to another man in another time. An inordinate length of belt with a succession of makeshift notches extended from the bunched up waistband of his baggy pants, evidencing the advancement of his condition.

As I looked across the room at this shell of a man, I wondered what set of choices and circumstances had torn him down to skin and bones, leaving him with the countenance of one who knew his days were prematurely numbered. I found myself making a judgment in my own mind about this man without benefit of any more evidence than my own assumptions. It was difficult for me to fathom the possible common link between this gaunt stranger and myself. Impulsively, a hostile resentment rose within; but then my heart softened, and I wondered if this man knew anything at all about the peace of God.

Erratic surges of fear prompted me to dwell on the issues at hand as I sat in my orange chair waiting to be called. All along, taking my cues from the media, I had had no reason to believe I was at risk. After all these years, the past belonged to the past—and none of it, I thought, related to me now. I really had not thought I was in any danger at all, but the doctor who spoke to me two weeks ago thought differently.

A nurse appeared to escort the thin man through a narrow corridor. I shivered as waves of hot and cold swept through my body. The temptation to jump up and walk out of the building mounted, but I stayed fixed in my chair and forced myself to concentrate on the absolutes: John 3:16, God loves me; Psalm 46:1, God is an ever present help in the time of trouble; 1 John 4:7, God loves Debi even more than I do, and he will surely enable her to go on without me if that is how it is to be. The title of a book, *Not Somehow, but Triumphantly*, came into my mind. With fresh determination, I thought, *Not somehow, but triumphantly*.

The voice of the nurse calling my receipt number brought my attention back into the room, and a sensation of queasiness took me rapidly back to "somehow." I stood and forced my legs to move in the direction of the nurse before she disappeared from sight. She walked without speaking down the narrow corridor darkened by closed doors on either side. As I followed her, I tried not to think, not to feel, not to anticipate the unknown. The weight of humiliation bore down on my heart, forcing an unliftable frown upon my face.

The nurse entered the room, indicating I should do the same. As she closed the door, my gaze wandered from the paper-laden desk pressed tightly into the corner to the medical paraphernalia spread across the Formica countertop and upward to the skeletal diagrams covering the walls. Two metal chairs took up most of the remaining floor space of this cube-sized room. Like the heartless arrows in the hallway, this room was void of warmth. I searched my mind for the calming images of the lush foothills I had seen earlier that morning, but the present scene was too dominant for me to successfully escape.

Carefully positioning herself and leaning forward just enough to present an attitude of concern, the nurse motioned me to face her and sit down.

"Hello, my name is Anna," she said. Her tone was polite and acceptable to me.

"Hello, my name is Sheila," I responded. After so many hours of silent monologue I had little desire to be overly talkative. If this lady named Anna was too abrupt with me I would leave, and if she was too kind, I would cry. There was a better chance of making it through if I could keep the balance.

"Before we go to the room across the hall, I'd like to make a few clarifications," she said. "First, we ask that you do not use full names during our conversation—either of yourself or of anyone else to whom you refer. And then I would like you to understand that I am here to answer any questions you might have. In a few moments we will take a sampling of your blood. But first, I would like to be sure you understand what this test is for."

She paused briefly, then scanned the form given to me by the receptionist.

"I notice here that you've marked yourself in the high risk category. Can you tell me why you believe you are at risk?" she asked.

"For thirteen years I was married to a man who was recently diagnosed as having AIDS," I said, scrutinizing her reaction as I spoke. Observing no subtle gestures of judgment, I relaxed my defenses a bit and went on with my explanation.

"I had called a doctor in my community to find out whatever I could about Bill's situation and life expectancy. Until I talked to the doctor, I had not known I was at risk. The doctor didn't know me or Bill. He suggested it was important for me to be tested to determine my status, for my own peace of mind. He said your office would be set up to do the test and protect my identity," I said.

"Do you know how the virus is transmitted?" the nurse asked.

"Yes, I believe so. From what I have heard, the AIDS virus can only be passed from one person to another through sexual contact or through the blood, as in receiving a transfusion or sharing contaminated needles. There are said to be documented cases of health-care workers coming into contact with the virus in isolated incidents," I answered. The nurse seemed to accept my answers, and she appeared to understand my deep apprehension. An alarming increase of new cases of AIDS (Acquired Immune Deficiency Syndrome) and of its forerunner, ARC (AIDS Related Condition), headlined the news in 1985. The San Francisco AIDS Foundation along with television station KPIX published the AIDS Lifeline series of brochures, providing factual information as the public's best defense against this rapidly progressing international health crisis. The Department of Public Health was moving quickly to accommodate people such as myself.

"Are there any questions you'd like to ask me?" she asked kindly.

"How long does it take for the test results to come back? And how will you notify me if you don't know who I am?" I asked.

"It will take about ten days for the results to come back from the lab. When you came in today the receptionist gave you a numbered receipt. That receipt is your only identification. On your way out, the receptionist will let you know the date to come back. Now, it is important to understand that you must return to this office in person on the date indicated with your numbered receipt. No one else can come in and pick up the results for you, and no information can be given over the phone. If you lose the receipt, it will be necessary for you to have another sampling of blood drawn. There are no exceptions to this procedure," she said with a stern finality. As soon as she felt she had made her point clear, she resumed a gentler attitude.

I was impressed that the health department placed a premium on the importance of confidentiality. From my perspective, they had made a wise choice in helping me, and hundreds of others like me, to take a responsible step without having to face insurmountable hurdles. The success of the testing program may very well rest in the ability of people to come from all walks of life without the added fear of being exposed before the facts are known.

The nurse and I talked a little longer, then we moved across the hall to another small room. She motioned me to sit down at a small desk that looked like it belonged in a school classroom instead of a treatment room. Anna wrapped a wide band tightly around my upper arm and in a brief moment drew an adequate amount of blood for the lab to test.

"There, that wasn't so bad was it?"

"No, I just get overly nervous," I said, relieved that it was over. "I feel a little lightheaded. May I sit here for a bit?" I asked as I sat back down.

"Of course. Sit here as long as you like. Why don't you place your head down on the desk until you're feeling better? I have another patient, so just leave when you're ready. Please pull the door closed when you leave," she said as she left the room.

As difficult as it was for me to take the HTLV 2 test, it was only the first step in the process. Next to come was the waiting—waiting to discover if this deathly virus had invaded my body as well. Six years had passed since I'd had any potential for coming in contact with the virus, and until two weeks ago, I had thought that was beyond the period of possible risk.

Up to this time, the recorded history of the disease seemed to indicate that the incubation period for the virus was limited to five years. However, the first documented cases of AIDS were still recent enough to give cause for concern on the part of the doctor. He had suggested that I take the AIDS test so I would know *for sure* whether or not I carried the virus.

Before long I was feeling well enough to notice the smell of the desk. One of the many "heads down" detentions inflicted on our fifth-grade English class flashed across my mind. I decided it was time to leave.

Outdoors, the fresh air replenished my strength and stabilized my shakiness. The midmorning traffic held to a comfortable flow as I drove home toward the valley. In the privacy of my car, I turned my heart toward God. "Thank You, God," I silently prayed, "for coming with me today. It hurts, Lord, and it humiliates me to my soul. But it had to be done, and You've kept me from cowering. Thank You! It makes me sad to think of what You've had to look upon in our little family these twenty years, Lord. Who could have thought our lives would come to this?"

As I drove for the next few miles, my mind journeyed through the calendars and pondered the circumstances leading to this traumatic day. I leafed back beyond weighted pages of wretched pain and broken, distorted images—back to the bright colors of carefree summers and the sweet memory of life when I thought of it as an open-ended adventure. It was the twelfth day of October, 1965.

LOOKING BACK   *Two*

Elevated by my expectations, I was only slightly affected by the authoritative demeanor of the American immigration officer.

"Place of birth?" he asked as he began to inspect the handful of documents I passed to him.

"Canada," I said, amused that he would ask me such a question when he held my Canadian passport in his hand.

"What is your age?"

"Twenty-three."

"Destination?"

"San Francisco," I replied, with a surge of excitement.

"Purpose of your visit and intended length of stay?" he asked.

"I plan to live and work in San Francisco for about one year."

"What is your status?"

"Permanent Resident," I said. It had taken a year to go through the process of applying for a green card. My entire life was investigated: my banking habits, my political views, my medical history. There were forms and more forms to be filled out and sent off to the Department of Immigration and Naturalization.

"Do you have family in the United States?"

"No, my family lives here in Canada."

"Have your belongings been declared?" he asked.

"Yes, my trunk is being loaded onto the train," I answered. Silence followed as he carefully inspected each document. Apparently satisfied, he looked up.

"Thank you, Miss Hood. Everything is in order. Please proceed quickly through the door to your right. Your train is about to depart," he said, with the slightest hint of a grin.

I boarded the train, and my excitement was as constant as the clicking of the wheels. Even the momentary sadness of saying good-bye to family and friends could not dampen my bright spirits for long. The passengers on the train were intriguing, as were the miles of trees and mountains and waterways passing by my window throughtout the course of the day. My assumption that twelve hours of gentle rocking would guarantee sleep at the end of the day was quickly proven false. The confined area in which I'd been sitting all day seemed to grow smaller as the light grew dimmer. The pitch-black night threw my reflection back onto the window as the haunting whistle, the ringing bells, and the flashing signals marked each little town on our journey south.

When morning came, I did my best to stretch my cramped muscles and to smooth my crumpled clothes. As soon as I was presentable, I entered the dining car for a welcome breakfast. I listened to the conversation going on around me, hoping to hear some talk of San Francisco. Was it actually warm in October? Were all the homes constructed like Victorian mansions, joined side to side for block after block? Were jobs plentiful and the people friendly? Were the streets decorated with flower vendors and cable cars? I was so sure it would be all of that and more. My vision of the future was as straight and as narrow as the track beneath our wheels.

The reasons people have for coming to the windy city by the bay are as diverse as the people who come. The sixties attracted the "free spirit," the Black Panthers, and the flower children. Sleek, black, chauffeur-driven limousines drove on the same road with grossly painted Volkswagen busses. Inverted crosses became distorted symbols of peace for the radical, while the credit card provided the symbols of success for the conventional. If there was a norm at all, it was to select a life-style and then yield to its dictates. Travel brochures spoke of soaring hills and clanging cable cars. The nightly news spoke of sit-ins and riots. And tourists poured in daily to catch a glimpse of this peculiar city's variety of sights.

San Francisco was, for me, simply another step in my efforts to see as much of the world as possible before settling down. The yearning to travel had begun to weave its way into my thinking in my early teens and persisted until it gained the strength of a tightly meshed net. Twelve months after graduating from a four-year term at the Vancouver School of Art, I took every dollar I'd so prudently saved, sent for my passport, and purchased an open-ended round trip ticket to New Zealand. Because my aunt and uncle, with whom I had lived since I was seventeen, believed my life choices were my own, I encountered no resistance to my plan to travel halfway around the world at twenty. The only contingency they held me to was that when I was down to my last fifty dollars, I board an ocean liner and return to Canada.

After eleven months of traveling throughout the South Pacific, I did just that. Living once again with my aunt and uncle, I began immediately to work, save, and map out my next adventure. Now Hawaii, Fiji, Tahiti, New Zealand, and the high divers of Acapulco were all behind me; Europe was ahead.

I was neither running away from anything nor running to anything. A year in San Francisco meant higher wages and the fulfillment of a travel plan. Growing up in the Canadian northwest, I developed an appreciation of the mountains and the sea and was therefore naturally attracted to the California coast. As the last traces of the Canadian Indian summer gave way to the cold bite of endless winter rain, I was particularly ready to absorb the warmth of the California sun.

The hour had finally arrived. The gentle rocking subsided as the train gradually creaked and hissed its way into the station. I mentally checked each of my carry-on items to be sure nothing was left behind. I was far too excited to be worried about any of the logistics of getting my belongings from point A to point B. Especially since I had no idea where point B was.

The view from the train station consisted of tracks, utility buildings and flatbed carts with large metal wheels. A blanket of clouds dimmed my expectation of the weather. I followed the crowd, stepping over rows of tracks before reaching the platform leading into a classic old building. From there we were ushered onto a bus displaying the words "San Francisco" in its upper window. A camaraderie developed among the passengers as we settled into our seats, crowded by our carried luggage. The train had come in at the Richmond station, and according to the driver, it would be about one hour before we reached the San Francisco city limits.

The bus took us on a freeway parallel to the bay. We could finally see the city as we approached a very large bridge with traffic on two separate levels. The anticipation of arriving at our destination overlapped the excitement of the journey, and I had to restrain myself from jumping about in childlike fashion.

The bus depot, located several blocks into the industrial segment of the city, held little appeal but served its purpose. The click of my heels on the floor echoed as I crossed the width of the room toward the exit sign. It was a happy day! With newspaper and maps in hand, I left the station in search of a place to live. The skyline in the distance gave me my bearings.

The "Apartment for Rent" section of the want ads was extensive enough to provide hope, and my desire to remain close to the downtown area provided the boundaries of where I would look. The harder part was determining the locations in which a young woman could safely live. One trip down to Eddy Street told me where the tenderloin district was. Geary Street, which ran directly into the center of the downtown shopping area, became my dividing line as I walked from one prospective address to another. Before the afternoon was spent, I had found a nice little place on upper Geary.

I felt good about the apartment I'd chosen, and I was oblivious to the fact that it usually takes considerably more time and effort to find such desirable living quarters at the meager amount my budget would withstand. The furnishing consisted of cheap Danish modern pieces and a bed that flung out of the wall. I thought it was great! The window overlooked a pool two stories below. Hungry, I decided to scout my new neighborhood before it became dark. I was sure I'd seen a small grocery store and a cafe that would be within easy walking distance, so I locked up my new home with a sense of satisfaction and went to see what I could find.

Having met the first challenge of finding a place to live, my adventuresome spirit moved on to the next challenge—finding a job. I rose early and walked down Geary Street toward the stores. Exclusive designs graced the windows of I. Magnin and Saks Fifth Avenue, their displays daring to place magenta next to red, and blue next to green. Union Square was alive with pigeons and people. This appeared to be the place to promote religious, political, and social causes. I had never seen such an array of weird extremes, and I found it hard to believe that it wasn't all just an exhibition, with placards and tambourines as accompanying props.

As I continued past Union Square in the general direction of the financial district, a poster in the window of an airlines office caught my attention. The memories of my previous experiences—driving wildly through the sugarcane fields of Fiji and sleeping in a grass hut with lizards flitting across the wall; viewing coral reefs through rich blue Pacific waters; standing by the gushing geysers of Rotorura listening to the music of the Maoris—continually spurred me on. Young and confident, I had a head full of dreams, and I was fortunate enough to be living them out.

By the third day in San Francisco, I had secured a job in a convenient location where I had the option of walking or taking the bus. Skinner, Hirsch and Kaye was a small company located on Kearny Street between Bush and Sutter. It dealt mainly in stereo and photo equipment and was proudly introducing Ampex's first video recorders for commercial use. My area of specialty would be with cameras and accessories. It was a family-owned business, and I was glad to work for them.

The city recaptured my fascination daily. The morning fog, which I repeatedly mistook for rain clouds, always managed to lift sometime during the morning. Cable car rides and shopping trips, Carmel and Sausalito, Chinatown and Fisherman's Wharf filled my weekends. Not long after arriving at my new job, life took on an added dimension of intrigue. The handsome, well-dressed, soft-spoken man who sold the Ampex recorders caught my attention.

He looked about thirty. His eyes were dark brown, his black hair was short and neat, and his clothes matched the professional look of the San Francisco businessmen crowding the financial district. His three-piece suits were always complemented by crisp, starched shirts and tastefully coordinated ties. Each morning he'd come through the door wearing a black cashmere overcoat. His hand would be clutching a black, crookneck umbrella—just in case the clouds didn't lift. It amused me how the infamous

San Francisco wind, which ruthlessly blew away the best of hairdos, had no adverse affect on this man's appearance at all.

Mrs. Skinner, our boss's wife, who derived more pleasure as a matchmaker than a bookkeeper, filled us in on the details of each other's identity.

"Now there's a man for you!" she declared, as she caught me glancing in his direction.

"No, I think he's a little out of my league," I said, embarrassed by her perceptive eye. "He looks so sophisticated and so much older."

"His name is Bill. He's single, and he just celebrated his thirtieth birthday earlier this month," she volunteered.

"But I have just turned twenty-three. That's seven years' difference!" I said.

"Oh, that's nothing," she responded, dismissing my protest. "You would be good for him."

It made me feel good that my new employer placed so much confidence in me, and it was fun to watch her attempts at bringing us together. Once we had been introduced, I was encouraged to note how Bill appeared in my work area with curious frequency.

Over the next two months, we just sort of watched each other throughout the day and talked superficially when we could between working. Gradually, we began to have coffee together, then lunches, then drinks and hors d'oeuvres after work.

Bill's air of sophistication matched that of the

people of the financial district. With the exception of a dear customer named Mrs. Lilienthal, our clientele had little tolerance for light-hearted small talk or spontaneous laughter, so it continually amazed me that Bill showed any interest in me at all. I knew I was drawn to his seeming maturity and refinement, but I had no idea what drew him to me.

We saw each other every day at work and almost every evening. We talked intensely for long hours, presenting our best sides to each other. Our conversation centered around our accomplishments of the past as well as things around us at the present. I learned that Bill was born in Detroit, had lived in Los Angeles, and had only recently come to San Francisco. His responses to personal inquiries were vague, suggesting that he considered these kinds of questions to be inappropriate. Instead, he spoke of his appreciation of the arts, and he was anxious for me to see the marble pieces he had sculpted. He loved the opera and addressed its masters by name with respect. I thought to myself, *I might grow into it—someday, maybe.* Connie Francis was more my style than Sutherland or Price. At least I could sing along to "Everybody's Somebody's Fool" without an interpreter.

In addition to the pull of Bill's physical attractiveness was the appeal of his soft-spoken manner and the diversity of his experiences. There was also something about his aloneness that drew me to him. We were both alone, and I thought I could fill a need for him just as he could fill a need for me.

Sometimes Bill would take me to a run-down movie theater or a questionable restaurant or bar, contradicting the image I had of him. But I brushed away any inclination to be suspicious or critical of his actions.

Thoughts of someday going to Europe grew dimmer as thoughts of settling down grew stronger. At the one and only dance Bill ever took me to, he asked me to marry him. Suddenly the prospect of a life partner held more appeal than traveling through life alone.

On Monday morning we announced our engagement to everyone at work. By now we had befriended the couple who owned the sandwich shop next door, so we eagerly shared our news with them when we took our morning coffee break. Mrs. Skinner was noticeably pleased, and she began immediately to assist me in the making of our wedding plans.

"Now, the first thing we need to do is set the date," she said, sounding more like my mother than my boss. "Are you planning to be married in the church, or are you going to go to Reno?"

"I definitely want to be married in a church," I said.

"Then you will need a wedding gown and a bridesmaid and champagne! Yes, I will call Petri's—he will supply the champagne. Who will give you away?"

"I don't know," I said, wondering aloud how many

members of my family would be able to make the trip down from Canada. "I've only just sent my letters off to let them know our news, so I shall have to wait till I hear back from them. I think my aunt and uncle will come. I've been living with them off and on over the past five years."

"What about your parents?" she asked.

"No, I just don't think they will come," I said, without offering any explanation.

When I was seventeen and just completing my second year of art school, my dad and I had had a difference of opinion. At that time, I could find no resolve but to pack my bag, say a quiet good-bye, and respond to my aunt and uncle's offer to live with them until graduation. Before coming to the States, my mum and I had arranged to meet for lunch in an effort to talk about our strained relationship. It was then I learned how much hurt my father had suffered when I left home, although he had never spoken of it. And although I had never spoken of it to my father, I had longed over the five years we'd been apart to have him come and take me back. Our differences were now settled, but we'd grown accustomed to living independently of one another.

"Well," she said as she pursued her own avenue of thoughts, "we will just have to settle on a date."

"June," I said. "I would like to be married in June."

"That doesn't give us much time, but we will begin at once, and it will all work out fine," she said. It had been less than a year since her own daughter's wedding, so the details of what we would need to do were fresh in her mind.

"Bill said the plans are up to me, and my funds are very limited, so I would like to keep it small but nice," I explained. I had absolutely no idea of what it would cost to have a wedding, and the thousand dollars I had to have in my account to qualify for my green card had already been partially spent on the purchase of a stereo for my apartment.

Bill and I did not discuss our finances, except to agree on opening a joint account. Since I was the only one with any savings, we added Bill's name to my account. He then went to Granat Brothers Jewelry and selected a beautiful pear-shaped diamond set in white gold for me to wear. And after talking with a pastor, we found April was the best time for him for the wedding date.

Mrs. Skinner kept her hand in my plans, and I enjoyed having someone to share in my anticipation. One day, when we were doing more talking than working, she asked me a question.

"Sheila, would you marry a man who had been married before?"

"No, I don't think so. I wouldn't want to be second best," I answered. "What made you ask me that?" It puzzled me that she had become so serious.

"Bill has been married before," she said. "I didn't think you knew."

"No, I didn't," I said, feeling my heart tighten within me. "He never said anything about being married before. How do you know that? When was he married? Why didn't he tell me?" I asked all at once.

"He probably didn't tell you because he didn't want to lose you," she said gently. "I think it was a long time ago, and it only lasted for a very short time. They were probably both far too young, and it just didn't work out."

"I just wish he would have told me," I said, still trying to digest this piece of unwelcome news.

"You must understand, Sheila, it was a long time ago, and I'm sure it was for the best that it ended," she offered in his defense.

"How do you know about it?" I asked.

"When he first came to work here, he told me. And now that you are about to be married, I thought you should know," she said.

"Thank you," I responded sadly.

"Will it make a difference to your plans?"

"I don't know. I want to talk to Bill."

"I just want the best for you, dear. But don't be too hard on him; I'm sure it was for the best," she said as she turned her attention to the pile of invoices in her hand.

Now that I was confronted with the issue, I questioned the basis for the way I was responding to the news of a previous marriage. Maybe it wasn't right to judge someone for something that happened ten years ago. Maybe Mrs. Skinner's counsel had some merit to it. After all, my own father had remarried after my mother had abandoned us when I was only two years old, and I was glad about it. Now that I had committed my heart to Bill, it wasn't so easy to make an unbiased decision.

But why Bill hadn't spoken of being married before puzzled me. So as soon as we got off work, I questioned Bill. His answer was very much the same as Mrs. Skinner's, and I was left to believe that it was a youthful decision that ended abruptly when his first wife left him. The protective side of me reasoned that she had wronged him by leaving. From that conclusion I decided to go ahead with our plans to get married.

KNEELING BEFORE THE ALTAR

Three

In April 1966, Bill and I were married at the First Baptist Church in San Francisco. Mrs. Skinner's daughter convinced me to wear her lovely satin and lace gown, and I had the baker make a three-tier fruitcake. My uncle agreed to give me away, and my sister stood in as my matron of honor.

Kneeling before the altar, I anticipated with delight our new life together as one. Directives to love, honor, and obey challenged my heart. These were not burdensome words, but sacred. It was the intent and the desire of my heart to give my all toward the fulfillment of the vows of that Palm Sunday afternoon. And as Bill soberly responded to the words of the pastor, I had every reason to believe his commitment corresponded to mine.

We left the church in a processional of streamers and blaring horns. Our reception was held at Bill's apartment, as it was now to become our new home. Located outside of the downtown area, its large, step-down front room and full dining room amply accommodated our small group of coworkers, family, and friends. With a huge kitchen, two oversized bedrooms, a second-floor studio, and roof access, Bill's apartment seemed to me to be quite large for just himself. When he explained that he'd had some roommates who had moved out about the time we began dating, it made more sense.

The afternoon was quickly spent. Storybook visions filled my head as we boarded the plane, bound for our honeymoon hideaway in southern California. Now, at last, resting against the shoulder of my new husband, I could relax and enjoy him. A wave of pride swept over me as I glanced down at our sparkling rings reflecting our commitment of unending love. Bill was unusually quiet, and he seemed to be preoccupied.

"Does flying bother you?" I asked.

"No, I'm fine," he said, matter-of-factly. His mood had changed radically. The sudden wall of indifference startled me. Throughout the flight, he gradually withdrew further and further into his own thoughts. My heart sank, and I wasn't sure how I was supposed to respond. Any romantic notions I had of capturing Bill's undivided attention in intimate conversation were abandoned when he began talking about a television program he wanted to see.

Little was said in the taxi that took us from the Los Angeles airport to our honeymoon suite. My heart sank even further when Bill announced his intention to stop off at his sister's and then at some favorite drive-in hamburger place. As the evening progressed, my disappointment pushed me to the point of defeat. The bright hope of the day turned into the agony of the night. I wanted to be alone with my husband, to be in the cherished center of his thoughts. Page by page, my storybook visions were blotted out, their life and color obliterated by black, gloomy strokes of rejection. What had I done to cause him to turn away from me?

I was deeply crushed. My dreams fell to the depths of my deflated being. The wedding vows so recently spoken echoed in my mind. As I sat alone in the bedside chair while Bill slept his way through our wedding night, I ached to understand his total rejection of me. *Perhaps it happens this way sometimes,* I thought. *Perhaps my expectation to be the object of my husband's desire was unreasonably high. Maybe tomorrow will be better.* But tomorrow came, and his desire was not for me.

During our brief three-month courtship, I had perceived Bill's lack of physical aggression toward me and assumed it was generated by respect and motivated by restraint. But now I was his wife and the need for restraint was gone. God and country agree that the marriage bed is pure, and I desperately wanted my new husband to want me. But he didn't.

We spent the remaining days of our honeymoon walking around Disneyland hand-in-hand. We appeared to be lovers, but we weren't. When I finally resorted to pleading, Bill gave in—but by then I felt cheated. Bill soon insisted on cutting our honeymoon short because he was worried about leaving our apartment unattended.

His disproportionate concern for the safety of our sparse furnishings bewildered me, as did the rest of his behavior. It had not appeared as though our neighborhood was particularly prone to vandalism. The white, steepled church directly across the street and the family-owned grocery store to its left had no bars on the windows, and the restaurant beneath our apartment serviced a pleasant-looking clientele of older folks. It didn't make sense to place more value on the security of a few things than on the security of each other. My only consolation was to look forward to the busyness of housekeeping to buffer my inward pain.

Gradually I began to realize how very little I knew about this man I had married. I had been so drawn by our mutual desire to spend quiet evenings talking together that I hadn't noticed how much of our conversation centered on past accomplishments. I was glad not to have to share him with his buddies. I attributed his lack of friends to his newness to the area, and his lack of money to his singleness and carefree living. After all, I had saved, spent, and traveled since graduating from school. Having money in the bank, I had reasoned, was only a means to a specific end. It never occurred to me to investigate further. Bill's explanations of particular circumstances in his life satisfied me. Taking people at face value, believing their words—that was how I lived.

We made our way through those early months. Sometimes Bill would give in to my pleas for intimacy. More often he would not. We still worked in the city together, and we still stopped at one lounge or another on the way home in the evening. When we arrived home, Bill would usually go upstairs to his studio. He preferred to be alone. He would join me for dinner, and then, as I did the dishes, he would go back to being alone until long after I had gone to bed.

Bill often referred to his need for space. There were times he'd insist on sending me home from work in a cab while he stayed in the city. I would plead with him not to send me home to an empty apartment while he went to nightclubs and bars, but I couldn't change his mind. He would promise to be along soon, but it was often far into the night before the sound of the key could be heard in the door.

Although Bill did not want to spend time with me, he gave me no freedom to acquire new friends, and he discouraged the old friendships I had made over the years. Gradually we became isolated, and the only place we saw the same people with any regularity was at work and at the sandwich shop next door.

When the sandwich shop opened, it was the first

of its kind in the San Francisco financial district and its new owners were outgoing, friendly people of wealth and stature. Pat, a former FBI agent, and his wife took on their new roles with a comfortable ease, magnetically drawing people in. Daily they spoke of their excitement with life and their love of God, and I decided at once that I liked their dynamic spirits. Like so many others who lined the block for a taste of Danish ham and Monterey Jack cheese piled high on a fresh, oversized onion roll, I was not disappointed with their fare.

But my greater interest was in what I heard them say about God. I began to challenge them with questions. They took the challenge and responded with Scripture verses. Every day I came in with new questions, and every day they sent me out with biblical texts to find and study. I dug out my old King James Bible from the bottom of my trunk and began to look for the verses. Many of them centered on the same gospel message I had heard as a young teen in our neighborhood church from a dear lady who had probably never stopped praying for me.

This process of learning continued until I came to a verse in the book of Luke that I couldn't get past: "Why call ye me, Lord, Lord, and do not the things which I say?" (Luke 6:46, KJV) At this point I knew there were no more questions I could ask. Now I was being questioned. Now God was challenging me. If I pressed on, ignoring the question confronting me, my spiritual quest would become insincere. Obedience to the verses I had committed to memory these past weeks had to be an integral part of my learning process if the truths of the Scriptures were to have meaning for me. I would need to take action.

One night in September, I sat alone and fought a battle within. On the one hand I could feel the pull of all I'd come to understand of God. On the other hand I could feel the pull of my own dreams and desires for my life. I began to consider following Jesus Christ as my Lord and Savior. But then I would fight to ignore this tugging in my inner being because I was afraid of what God might expect of me.

In addition, my confidence in my ability to make good choices had dropped considerably over the past year. Somehow I knew that if I decided to follow Jesus, to become a Christian, it would be a life-changing choice. I wasn't so sure I could do whatever it was that God would be asking of me, so I thought maybe I should leave well enough alone. Yet I had great difficulty with that line of thinking because my life was empty. Even with a partner, I was going through life alone.

Dreams were vanishing; possibilities had turned into impossibilities. Nothing had real purpose. My own standard was all I had to live by, and that wasn't enough. The philosophies of the times left me cold. I desperately felt the need to be loved unconditionally. God offered me that kind of love through His Son who had died for me on the cross of Calvary. I needed hope, and God offered a purpose and a plan and eternal security. Although I wrestled with the options before me, in the end, I accepted God's gift of salvation.

I humbly knelt before God and declared my belief in Him and in His Word. Not entirely sure where to begin, I decided to rehearse the Bible verses I had recently learned:

> For God so loved the world, that he gave his only begotten Son, that whosoever believeth in him should not perish, but have everlasting life. For God sent not his Son into the world to condemn the world; but that the world through him, might be saved (John 3:16-17, KJV).... There is none righteous, no, not one.... For all have sinned, and come short of the glory of God (Romans 3:10, 23, KJV).... If we confess our sins, he is faithful and just to forgive us our sins, and to cleanse us from all unrighteousness, (1 John 1:9, KJV).... I am the way, the truth, and the life; no man cometh unto the Father, but by me (John 14:6, KJV).

I prayed, "This is what I've come to understand of You, God. I know I am a sinner, and I ask You to forgive me. I thank You for sending Jesus to die for my sins, so that I could come before You today and receive forgiveness and eternal life, and hope and peace. I believe Jesus died on the cross. I believe He died and was buried. And I believe that on the third day He rose victorious. Thank You, God! Amen."

I rose from my knees a Christian. In the heart of the city, in the heart of the sixties, I became a child of the living God. The seed of new life had been planted.

Later in the same month of September 1966, another seed of life was planted—our first and only child. Becoming a Christian and a mother changed my perspectives and filled my life once again with excited anticipation. With the helping hand of God, old habits, including living according to my own goals, were gradually replaced with God-honoring ways, and the hunger to learn more of the God whom I now served increased. Awaiting the birth of our baby, I enrolled in an extensive Bible correspondence course.

Bill was also being ministered to through our friends at the restaurant. His struggles and responses were of a different nature than mine, and there were times when instead of letting go of the nightlife and its companions, he would simply incorporate religion into his worldly life-style, making us both unhappy. Other times he would respond to the challenge to be "sold out to Jesus Christ" by separating himself even further from me to pray at length and read the Scriptures. I was both elated and confused by his behavior because of its extremes.

As Bill continued to give the Christian life a concerted effort, we began attending an evangelical church. After a number of months we were both baptized, giving public testimony to our private decisions to die to self and live for Christ. When our beautiful daughter, Debbora, was born, we dedicated her to God, vowing to raise her in His ways and in His love.

Hope began to grow in me that our family life would soon be better. Clinging to the belief that it would be just a matter of time before Bill would want to become a biblically defined husband who loved me as Christ loves the church, I looked beyond his indifference to me, his long hours of brooding, and the times out for which he gave no accounting. I looked optimistically for the day when he would be free of the constant inner turmoil and puzzling imbalances of his daily life. As his moods changed, so did his convictions. He would vacillate from being dogmatic and highly regulated to being obnoxious, erratic, and worldly.

Bill was a talented, capable person who could sculpt and draw with excellence. My four years at the Vancouver School of Art were no match for his natural ability to bring a sketch of a person to life with a handful of pencils. I could study the Scriptures all day and never dig as deeply into its well of understanding as he did. He seemed able to excel in anything he chose to do.

But the dark side of Bill was as extreme. He could think thoughts and do deeds that would surely touch the very gates of hell. No matter how serene his environment, anger rumbled beneath his meticulous surface like a volcano about to erupt. Living with Bill's changeable personality was like living with Dr. Jekyll and Mr. Hyde. As his thoughts and deeds unpredictably swung from the gentle to the grotesque, it was like facing two opposing enemies bent on destroying each other. Only behind the closed doors of our home was the double life of Bill explicitly seen.

And so we went back and forth, hoping and despairing—and always praying. I prayed, and I believed that if I just kept on praying, one day we would become a united, fulfilled family with faith, freedom, and wholeness bonding our marriage. I could only assume Bill's desire was the same as mine. I felt sure of it when we finally began to talk together of the steps we would need to take to become dedicated, committed Christians. Time would reveal whether or not my assumption was correct.

THE STRAIN OF CONFESSION

Four

Bill changed jobs and took positive steps of commitment. He began to study the Bible and to speak of serving God. Encouraged by our friends at the sandwich shop, we became acquainted with the ministry of Christian Women's Clubs (CWC) and its founder, Helen Baugh. We met Helen for lunch after she and her associate, Mary Clarke, invited us to attend a CWC conference in Santa Rosa. Bill and I were unsure of the outcome of this meeting, but we were united in our readiness to respond. So when we received the invitation to come and fill the positions of photographer and artist at the national headquarters in Kansas City, Missouri, we accepted.

Over the next three months, we made arrangements for our move to Missouri. We were met at the airport by Myrtle Baron, a hospitable and gracious lady who ushered us through the airport to her waiting car. My notion that air conditioners were extravagant accessories was promptly revised as we struggled to acclimate ourselves to the humid, oven-hot air. As we drove along the tree-laden streets toward the headquarters (more commonly referred to as "Stonecroft"), my heart confirmed that serving God in a full-time capacity was my highest aspiration. Believing Bill's vow to abandon his old ways, I felt unencumbered and eager to plunge into the task before us.

The car slowed as we approached the arched entry. The name *Stonecroft* etched into its stones confirmed we'd reached our destination. Forty acres serenely encompassed the master house. In close proximity to one another, the staff apartments and office complex sat nestled among huge old trees. The distant orchard showed promise of a plentiful harvest, and rows upon rows of garden vegetables abundantly fed large numbers of residents and guests. Captivated by the beauty, we were warmly welcomed and rapidly adjusted to living and working in this wonderful setting.

Bill's capabilities—taking pictures, developing and stripping negatives, and other publication skills—were put to full use, while I concentrated more on the areas of layout and design. It was an ideal working situation for both of us, and much of my work was done at home so I could spend ample time with

Debi. Although I had not yet realized she was to be our only child, I had become aware that she was a special gift from God. Her warm, responsive spirit would delight anyone's heart.

The penetrating heat of summer eventually gave way to a blaze of vivid autumn colors. The leaves fell to the ground and were gently, quietly covered with a myriad of perfectly formed flakes of snow.

I grew in my faith, and a peace permeated my being. But as my sense of well-being accelerated, so did my sense of concern about Bill. Since our arrival at Stonecroft, his outward, public behavior fit tightly into an acceptable pattern, but inwardly he was always angry. It wasn't a boisterous, physical anger, but a deep, constant undercurrent that I couldn't understand.

The winter not only brought the magnificent beauty of untouched snow, it also brought the dreaded Hong Kong flu. Debi came down with it, followed by Bill, then myself, then Debi again. Through the lengthy periods of recuperation, I found myself weighted down with the elements of our relationship over the past two years. Even though our life together seemed a little better now, there were few soft colors forming on the picture in my mind. Much of what I saw was harsh and painful to look back on—the disappointment of our wedding night . . . endless nights of rejection . . . nights when I stood at the window until morning waiting for Bill to come home. I remembered the stark horror written on the face of one of Bill's friends when I showed him my engagement ring and recalled how ill-at-ease it had made me feel.

"God," I prayed aloud as I lay on my bed alone, "what is wrong with our lives? We should be so content living and working here in Your service. This place is so beautiful, the people here are so gracious, our work is so appreciated. But it's us, God. There is something very wrong with us. Am I so ugly that my husband never wants me? Or is it something else? Something deeper? God, I'm scared to even think it . . . but I can't get away from it. Please, God, help me to see straight, to think straight. I feel so desperately alone. Bill is always angry, and the pain is endless, and there are a number of things I've been pushing out of my mind. They are like red flags of warning—the bottle of perfume in his shirt pocket . . . the times he'd try to slip his wedding ring back on unnoticed after an especially late night in the city . . . the way his eyes met with those of total strangers . . . the preoccupation he has with his outward appearance that has nothing to do with pleasing me. Lord, with so many days to lie here and think and with so little energy to fight, I need Your help. I need to confront Bill with the conclusions I'm perceiving. Please help me, Lord."

Still shaky from the effects of the flu, I got up slowly and went into the other room to find Bill and confront him. My heart pounding and my hands icy,

I silently rehearsed the words I was about to say. I hesitated momentarily in the doorway, realizing that if my conclusions were wrong, Bill would get terribly angry and withdraw from me even more—and if they were right he might slump into unbearable silence. I had to push myself to say the thoughts that could no longer be contained.

"Bill, there's something I must ask you." I paused to take a deep breath as if it would give me an added measure of courage. "Bill, what is it that keeps you angry inside? And what is it that keeps you at a distance from me day after day and night after night? Is there something deeply wrong?"

At first he said nothing—he just stared, without expression. Finally, he broke the incredible silence.

"Yes, Sheila," he said, breaking under the strain of confession.

"What is it, Bill?" I was afraid of what I was about to hear because by now my heart seemed to know what his words were going to confirm.

"Yes, there's something I haven't told you. I have this terrible battle raging inside of me all of the time. It's not against you. It's just that I, well, it's just that I prefer to be with men."

"Do you mean intimately, sexually?" I asked, feeling my heart crushing inside me.

"Yes," he said as he lowered his gaze toward the floor. "But not since we came to Stonecroft—not the deeds, anyway . . . just the thoughts. I can never get away from the thoughts."

The implication of his words sank in slowly. "You mean you've been involved sexually with men since we were married?" I asked. The tears were hot on my face, and I trembled at the thought of it. "Why should you want someone else when you didn't even want me?" I blurted out. "Why on earth did you marry me? What could have caused you to make such choices?" Bringing myself to think of what he did when he was with men was more than I wanted to do, and it was beyond the regions of my understanding to know why he wanted to do it. What I did understand was that this problem was corroding our marriage, and it was destroying Bill.

Weakened by the depth of our conversation, I sank into the chair. Bill seemed almost as perplexed as I did about his circumstance, and neither of us felt equipped to deal with his inner struggles.

Believing God can heal anything, I made the decision to stand by Bill in the days to come. Right or wrong, I trusted that fervent prayer would put this problem behind us. Occasionally Bill would join me in asking God to free him from this gripping entanglement.

In his own mind he considered his actions to be a violation against himself and against God. He neither qualified nor justified his choices. He didn't consider himself to be homosexual or even bisexual; he considered himself to be participating in homosexual activity, strongly resisting any form of titling for his behavior. This differentiation is one on which he never varied. Never did Bill claim the secret life he lived was OK with God. In fact, he admitted the great battles he fought within were between his love for God and his lust for men. He knew that what he was doing was detestable. He read it in the Scriptures. He knew it in his heart.

My initial response of anger and repulsion subsided as I sensed Bill's brokenness over his past. Sometimes it was confusing to know what to do with the information his confession provided, but somehow I knew I could tell no one. Bill continued spending long hours alone, and we went along doing the best we could.

Before our first year at Stonecroft came to an end, Bill announced his decision to leave. Because the hidden segments of Bill's past were an ever-present concern, and because I did not want us to be responsible for bringing any form of disgrace upon the work of the gospel, I did nothing to hinder his decision.

In February we sold our furnishings, purchased a car, and having said our good-byes, passed back through the stone archway. We reasoned to ourselves that isolation from the "real world" would have caused us to leave eventually anyway. But secretly, as the final corner was hidden from view, I wished I could have stayed there forever.

With youthful optimism, we rebounded into idealistic plans for the future. Bill was sure he could find a job in San Francisco and add considerably to the minimal wages of the past year, and I anticipated staying home with Debi. We seldom talked of what we were leaving behind but drove along silently, respecting each other's need to reconcile from within. I found consolation in the feeling deep inside me that said we were doing the right thing and that God would take care of us if we were obedient to Him.

After several weary days of driving, we relocated in the city of Alameda just across the bay from San Francisco. As I had hoped, I was able to be at home with Debi while Bill commuted into the city, and the newness of things kept us preoccupied. We contacted our Christian friends from the restaurant and began attending Redwood Chapel Community Church in nearby Castro Valley. As far as I knew Bill had not resumed any of his old relationships. We took time out to visit my aging grandfather in Canada, and I shared my newfound faith with him.

As we made the return trip home, Bill began to speak of his desire to attend a Bible college. We had both come to realize our need for a more solid foundation, and schooling appealed to both of us. Bill was spending more time with us now, and his ups and downs were not as frequent or as extreme of late. I so much wanted to get on with our lives, and at last Bill seemed to want to as well. Upon the recommendation of our friends, we applied and were accepted at Dallas Bible College in Mesquite, Texas, for the upcoming fall semester. It meant another long drive back across country, but the anticipation of what was ahead kept it from becoming a burden.

RADICAL CHANGES

Five

Once again miles from the cool, ocean breezes, I had to become acclimated to the temperatures and the humidity. Debi and Bill adjusted more readily than I did, which was fortunate for them. The red Texas sun pressed its way up over the horizon at the earliest hour of the morning, just daring anyone to stand in its rays. We moved into a nice, new apartment only a block or so from school. Bill registered for classes. One of the staff wives agreed to care for Debi, and I began my new job at the Central American Mission. Bill also took a job at the nearby Big Town Shopping Center in Mesquite.

Everything was falling into place. Now the evenings were spent typing assignments and trying to keep the house in order. We joined the Scofield

Memorial Church, and I began to teach Sunday school to the first-grade children. Debi invited Jesus into her tender, three-year-old heart.

By his second year, Bill's grades declined. We concluded it would be a help if I gave up my job and attended classes with him. The more involved I became, the more aloof he became. He wasn't interested in his studies or in any form of Christian service (even though it was part of his class assignment). His grades dropped far beneath his ability. Familiar old patterns of anger and withdrawal resurfaced. He became forceful, unkind, and extremely negative. Realizing that it wasn't an encouragement to him to have me attend school, I completed the semester, then went back to work.

Late one afternoon, as I helped Debi in the door with her bag of toys, my eyes were drawn to a note in Bill's handwriting propped on the kitchen table. "Did not go to work today. Am not going back to school. Bill." My heart sank. For three days and nights we waited for some word from Bill. I had no idea where he would go, but as soon as the bank opened, I knew he wasn't without funds. He'd taken all our money, including the inheritance my dear grandfather had left to me.

Although we attended church and school, there was no one in the whole state of Texas for me to confide in. I couldn't tell my family because I couldn't reveal Bill's secret. And now I was sick, angry, and scared. I had no money, nothing. What was a mother alone with a three-year-old girl supposed to do? I helped Debi with her dinner, put her into her pajamas, then went to my room and cried. I fumbled my way through the days and the nights until the phone finally rang. Bill was at the airport and wanted me to pick him up. He'd flown to and from San Francisco.

My feelings were a mixture of relief and hurt. As I groped my way through the unfamiliar, pitch-black streets to the airport, I had to wonder what hold Bill had on me. He had treated me so badly, yet I still felt compelled to come and get him. Maybe I felt sorry for him, or maybe I was afraid of him—or afraid of being left alone.

Once again, his profuse apologies remedied the situation at hand. But another dream was crumbling. Our college days ended, unfinished, and we drove back to California because we preferred living there.

Somewhere along our trail of unfinished commitments, Pat and his wife, the couple who had been so important in sharing the gospel of Christ's love with us, withdrew their friendship. I assumed we hadn't made the grade, that we just were not good enough Christians. So instead of the Bay Area, we settled in San Diego.

Moving around ceased to be an adventure for me. I was weary of the changes in plans and in moods. I was weary of having no security. And most of all, I was weary of being rejected and lonely. We didn't leave friends behind because we didn't make them.

Bill had his own life to live. And I, being his wife, was subjected to it—even when he was verbally abusive and controlling. I had made a commitment to love, honor, and obey. So I kept it.

Sin is not exclusive to any given geographical location. Bill had no difficulty living out his fantasies wherever he went. By now I was losing confidence in him, in myself, and in the God who said He would be my friend. My problem was that I didn't know how to appropriate His promises. I had never been so sad and so miserable. And being a Christian only increased my sadness. I gave in to my feelings of defeat because I kept expecting God to change Bill and our marriage. I thought God had given me no other alternative than to submit to Bill in obedience. And I also was burdened with an added sense of failure because I didn't think we were acceptable Christians. When we came to southern California, we didn't bother to look for a church. My Bible lay unopened in a box somewhere. I no longer wanted to talk to God.

Through the assistance of an FHA subsidized loan, we bought a house in the newly developed area of Mira Mesa. I worked in the home while Bill traveled into downtown San Diego. For a while we were busy putting up fences, wallpapering rooms, and laying the foundation for the additional room Bill wanted to build. With his heel to the dirt, he cleverly designed the landscaping of the front yard.

I tried not to cry as Debi and her new friend

proudly stood for pictures on their first day of kindergarten. I found it threatening to entrust her to a stranger who wouldn't love her and watch out for her as much as I did. I felt a little like I was losing her and the comfort of her company.

As I then concentrated on our home and it developed a welcome warmth, I was sure it would cause Bill to want to return to it at the end of his working day. I was wrong. Under the guise of going night fishing, he would walk in the door, pick up his gear, and be gone—off into the night to pursue his desires. Sometimes he made less effort to conceal where he was going.

Even now I never really wanted to believe what I suspected to be true of his activities. Bill was an excellent master of deception, and I was a gullible target. I wanted to believe the best. My motive was probably more selfish than noble. Sometimes I think I chose to believe him because I wanted a good marriage.

Some radical changes began to take place. Bill's taste in music switched from classical opera to acid rock. His powerful speakers blasted sounds that were crass and offensive into our quiet neighborhood, causing me irritation and embarrassment. His attitude and his language pierced my heart. His habitual drinking, which had actually begun long before I knew him, increased and, with it, irresponsibility.

On the one hand, Bill seemed bent on self-destruction; on the other hand, he spent countless hours meticulously caring for his beautifully landscaped garden. He painted Disney scenes on Debi's walls that would have impressed a critic. But then, at the most unpredictable moments, he would set down his tools and be gone. Watching Bill do the worthy, constructive things made it all the harder to comprehend the deliberately ruinous ones.

All his promises to reform were made the "day after." With the smell of alcohol still dripping from his pores, Bill would ask me to forgive him; and I did. Remorse was a predictable element of the scenario. I would beg him to forsake his drinking and his sexual sin, and he would assure me it was a part of the past. He would change his clothes and shower and replace his wedding ring on his finger. I would prepare some food for him to eat. Then, in a few days, it would happen all over again.

Some losses hurt more than others. The decision to sell our lovely home after three short years was one of my more painful disappointments. It was not an issue of possessions; it was an issue of security. I just had not thought we would move again.

This time, Bill's search for adequate employment and affordable property took us to Montana. It was cold and lonely and I hated it there. Bill bought ten acres of land on the old "Bootlegger Trail." The frozen soil was solid clay. Abandoned coyote traps lay in wait, ready to clamp the foot of any unsuspecting foe, be it man or animal. The realtor's "beautiful pond" was nothing more than a lure for all manner of snakes. Bill's directive that Debi and I should always wear skirts or dresses for the sake of appearances compounded our distaste for the cold. Shortly after our move, while Bill was down in Santa Rosa getting our stored belongings, Debi and I were caught unaware in a blizzard. Inadequately dressed for the unexpected storm and miles from home, we huddled and shivered and feared for our life. The car we were in was stuck at the edge of a steep embankment. By the time we were rescued from the ice and snow and freezing temperatures, my fear had changed to anger. I hated it there even more.

Finally I summoned the courage to tell Bill I was done with passively following him all over the country. I earnestly begged him to take us back to California. At least there, when he left us alone, we wouldn't die of the elements. Riding on the same boost of courage, I purchased pants for myself and leggings for Debi.

Bill gave in to my begging, and we left immediately for the nerve-racking trip south in the dead of winter, pulling the nineteen-foot travel trailer that now served as our home. Uncertain of our destination, I knew I did not want to go to Mira Mesa because I couldn't bear to see some other family living in our house. Maybe we could move farther out into the unincorporated area east of San Diego. Maybe we could still buy a small piece of land. Bill dreamed of building his own house. Perhaps now.

THE WORST DAY *Six*

The day began with a notable sameness. Lakeside had a rustic beauty, and we felt we'd done well purchasing this acre of land so comfortably nestled at the base of the El Capitan Mountains. The soil beneath our feet was rich with the residue of the San Diego riverbed. Bill particularly enjoyed tending the raised plots of melons and vegetables that he'd planted at the earliest opportunity. The quietness of the morning was occasionally interrupted by the whinny of a horse, or the squawk of a flustered hen fleeing from our young dog, Blue. These were familiar country sounds to the folk in this unincorporated area.

In the year previous to our coming, the land had produced a robust crop of watermelon. The rich green carpet of oats had barely risen beyond the height of a good healthy lawn when we first negotiated to buy; ultimately it produced forty-nine large bales of oat hay. We sold the hay to a nearby boarding stable, and Bill began to prepare to build.

We pulled our nineteen-foot travel trailer onto the property near the south end next to the garden. The corral for Debi's horse was built at the north end, and the markers for our country-style, natural wood home were set back from the easement road very near to the center of the property.

The prospect of building our own home was an exciting one. We'd have open space around us and a panoramic view reminiscent of days gone by. I stood where the kitchen was to be and looked out to the old, weather-worn barn on the adjacent ranch, feeling a surge of excitement as I captured the dream. Beyond the ranch, the sparsely used highway unobtrusively came into view, then rose to disappear into the heart of the mountain. I felt a deep satisfying pleasure in the natural work of God's hand quietly surrounding me.

My soul-felt serenity abruptly dissipated as I glanced over in the direction of the corral. Bill was leaning on the rail talking to Debi's black Welsh pony. It's difficult to define how I knew when Bill was about to leave for the bar in town. An air of restlessness perhaps. My heart sank as he made his way to the car. Without any word he drove off down the easement road as he'd done so often before. There'd be no building today.

I didn't know exactly where he went or what he did when he left. Drinking was certain. It would be three or four in the morning before he'd return. Forcibly, I covered my anguish for fear the neighbors would detect what was going on. The frequency of Bill's trips into town had increased. Anguish and fear became my companions. Loneliness penetrated my heart, and my mind was filled with confusion. But as friendless and wounded as I was, I did not consider leaving.

I reasoned that keeping busy would help. I knew that too many thoughts of Bill's excessive habits and deceptive ways could easily overwhelm me. The remaining monies from the sale of our house were rapidly dwindling, and Bill was making no effort toward finding employment. I decided to sew in an attempt to change my focus.

Debi had entered her first horse show and was still in need of a riding outfit. Some material that I had on hand was a pleasing shade of pink and would provide a sharp contrast to the deep coloring of her horse. The pink would also help to show off Debi's long, blonde hair and accentuate her rosy skin under the protection of her wide-brimmed hat.

It was too hot to sit in the trailer, so I brought the sewing machine outside and carefully measured the fabric to be sure I had enough to fit Debi's seven-year-old frame. Debi was such a pretty girl, and it gave me a sense of satisfaction to make her clothes for her. Perhaps being busy making something she needed would serve as a remedy to my wounded spirit. I refused to think about what bar Bill might be at or why he went in the first place. It only added pain upon pain. Sewing seemed like a beneficial alternative.

It was well into the afternoon when I heard the sound of an unfamiliar car coming down our easement road. I did not recognize the man who stepped out a few feet away from where I sat sewing. His manner was abrupt and I immediately felt myself being intimidated by him.

"Does Bill live here?" he asked.

"Yes . . . yes, he does," I responded. A wave of sick fear surged over me.

"Does he drive an El Camino?"

"Yes," I said, more in a question than a statement. My heart began to pound. *Who is this man? What does he want?* I thought to myself. When at last he announced he'd come from the car dealership to reclaim the car, I was almost relieved. Immediately my relief was replaced with humiliation. Bill was supposed to have been making payments.

"I'm sorry, Bill isn't home. I don't know when he'll be back. If the car were here you could take it. But it's not, and I don't know what to tell you," I said nervously. In the same abrupt manner in which he came, the man left. My family in Canada had not had a lot of possessions, but what we did have was respectfully ours. A heaviness lingered over me like an unliftable weight. Again, I pushed myself back to sewing.

The easement road was about the equivalent of a standard city block. It was a private road with only four properties accessing it, making the traffic predictable. Half an hour later, a white car with an indistinguishable green emblem on the door passed by. Numbly I stared down the road as yet another unfamiliar car finally turned in and eased to a stop in front of the picnic table.

"Pardon me, ma'am," the driver said, stepping out of his car. He was a kindly looking man with a gentleness in his voice. By now the emblem on his car door was fully legible. "I'm from the Health Department. I've come to tell you to be moved off your property within ten days. The house plans you submitted have not been picked up and the septic tank must be in for you to remain living in your trailer. Why hasn't your husband come to pick up the approved plans?" His words ran together in my ears as he carried out his allotted responsibility. But his eyes were filled with a mixture of puzzlement and compassion.

I found some comfort in this gentle man's genuine regret at having to evict us from our land. He said a few more words, got back into his car, and drove away. I walked over to the portion of land marked off for the trench which would have girded the foundation of our home. There, I hung my head and wept. Our little dream house would never be built. Bill handled his money—our money—to his own advantage, employing schemes of persuasion and evasion. Next to his rejection of me, his lack of financial integrity was the biggest drain on my dignity and self-worth. If our word wasn't our bond, if our signature wasn't our trust, then how could we hold our heads up in the community—or in the mirror? How could we hope to build and find roots on such an unsure footing?

By the time a Sears van pulled up an hour later on that same afternoon, my responses were almost mechanical. After a brief confrontation concerning Bill's delinquent account, I realized I again was dealing with a reasonable man, and we worked together on an agreeable solution. I felt the inequities of being held responsible for the deeds of an irresponsible person—responsible and, to my great dismay, liable.

I could not rid myself of the pressing weight on my shoulders. Bill's way of life was stripping us down to nothing. I was mortified. It was useless now to try to sew. Debi would be home from the neighbor's soon. I needed to regain my composure and think about preparing dinner.

"Where's Papa?" she asked as the two of us sat down to eat.

"He's in town, Debi," I said.

"Is he drinking again, Mama?" she asked.

"Yes, I think so, Sweetie," I said, trying hard to cover the pain the day had brought me.

"Mama, why did you make Papa go and drink? Why, Mom?" she asked. I was shocked by her question.

"What do you mean? Whatever has made you think it is my fault?"

"Because I saw you, Mama . . . I saw you throw away all of Papa's drinks yesterday. So it's your fault he had to go and get more," she said.

"Oh, Debi, it's all so hard to explain. Please trust me, Debi, and please, please don't blame me," I said.

Sensing my feelings, she ran to me with her accepting arms open for a forgiving hug. She had thrown a scare into me such as I'd never experienced before. Her countenance echoed her reluctance to be my accuser. Even as I poured out the bottles of Vodka stashed in the shed and over near the corral, I had wondered at the wisdom of my action. It was Bill's customary habit to confine his choice of liquor to beer. Only occasionally would he add hard liquor because it made him violently ill and more inclined toward violent behavior; and so I did what I could to prevent the reaction.

"Come on, Deb, let's just eat and get ready for bed," I said. The nights out on the property were intensely dark, and tonight I felt especially vulnerable.

Lying in my bed, I was thankful to hear the slow, even breathing telling me Debi was sleeping. The smallness of the trailer kept us only a few feet apart. She liked her bunk, and I was glad to have her near. Wishing sleep would come, I was suddenly startled by rustling noises directly beneath the trailer—directly beneath my bed. In helpless horror I listened as our dog killed the neighbor's prize rooster. It kept squawking and squawking and squawking. And I had no idea what to do. The dog had just wandered in one day and stayed, but it maintained its distance and did not respond to instruction. It was not much more than a pup, but it didn't seem safe—or even possible—to crawl under the trailer and pull his prey from his mouth. It was awful because I wanted to help, and I just couldn't.

At last, silence. The rooster was dead. I had not even tried to save him because I was sure my attempts would fail. I was failing so much. It burdened my soul.

At two o'clock in the morning, which was earlier than usual, Bill returned. He was drunk and belligerent. I was indignant and humiliated and worn by the events of the day. We argued. He threw a heavy ashtray which bounced precariously from wall to wall, then tore open the door and went outside.

Rushing over to Debi, I took her from her bed still wrapped in her blankets and made my way toward the car. I decided we'd taken all we could take. I was not going to subject myself—or Debi—to any form of physical violence. The emotional abuses had already ripped open my heart.

Adjusting to the darkness, I fearfully scrambled into the car and started the engine. Bill defiantly stood directly in front of us. He pounded on the hood of the car. Then he made his way along the fender, banging as he went. Debi was wide awake and horrified. Instinctively I knew it was best to shut off the car and go back in the trailer. Best, at least, as far as our immediate safety was concerned. Bill stepped to the side as I got out of the car and pulled Debi close to me. He then staggered into the car, slammed the door, and screeched out into the night.

Alone again, I calmed Debi and put her back into her bed. Never had I felt so low. Never had I sensed such a total inability to handle either myself or the situation in which I found myself day after day. The growing weight on my back was crippling me. I literally fell to my knees and cried out to God.

"God," I stammered. "I can't . . . I just can't handle it! I always thought I could. I thought that if I just tried hard enough, I could handle it. But I can't. It's all gotten too hard. And too miserable. I'm really scared, God. I'm scared for me, and I'm scared for Debi. What's going to become of us? How could our life have gotten to be such a mess?

"My head has such a pressure in it that it feels as though it'll split open. It feels like an ocean wave swelling up with no place to break and level off. God, my heart aches and wrenches inside me. Please, God, please, take this whole terrible mess and handle it for me. I beg You, Lord, please take the burden off my back," I prayed.

Limp and emotionally exhausted, I got up from my knees, crawled into the empty bed, and slept at once.

What I had asked God to do was to lift the load.

Bill still drank every day. He still resisted looking for a job. The eviction was firm. And we were still greatly in debt. But somehow, that's how I expected it was going to be. The great healing difference came from the realization that God had taken the weight of my load. He'd heard my prayer, and I was learning to walk again.

FALTERING STEPS OF FAITH

Seven

A year passed. We lived in a trailer park in El Cajon, not too far from Lakeside. We sold the property, Debi's black pony, Beauty, and then the trailer. Bill drank constantly. He didn't bother to even try to find work. Often Debi and I were left alone. As long as we had the property, I had been able to sell our fruit and vegetables to pay for our trailer space at the travel park.

After we sold our land, I was hired to teach during intersession, a periodic three-week session, at a year-round elementary school. Arrangements were made to enroll Debi, and we went off to school together. A heart's desire was being fulfilled. Teaching was a profession I highly regarded. My responsibilities included teaching puppetry, art, photography, and stitchery with a bicentennial theme. We were in a pilot program attempting to solve the problem of overcrowding in the country school. I loved my job and the people I worked with. And I knew Debi felt a security in being there with me.

Still, we made no friends. Our life was a perpetual cover-up. The uplift that came from my job was quickly snuffed out when we came home in the afternoon. We depended on Bill to meet us after the school bus dropped us off about ten miles from home. The day I had to take Debi's hand and walk the distance, while Bill sat in some bar, I felt myself taking the weight of the burden as I'd done so often in the past. We had no money, and it wouldn't have helped anyway because there wasn't any public transportation that far out. The afternoon sun beat down on us without mercy. I was too afraid to allow a stranger to give us a ride. So we just walked.

Salty tears spilled from my eyes. Debi clenched my hand tightly and kept herself from complaining about her tired little legs. As the desperateness began to well up, I thought about God. As we walked, we prayed through our tears that God would get us home before we collapsed from the heat.

When we sold the trailer, we moved into a duplex. One rainy, winter evening, I poured Harvey's Bristol Creme into a small crystal glass. It was not often that I drank, nor in excess. A single glass on a cold evening now and again was all. I could feel Debi's gaze and was surprised by the depth of sadness in her questioning eyes.

"Mama, why is it all right for you to drink alcohol and not for Papa?" I was startled by her question.

"It's not the same, Debi," I said. "It's not the same—your daddy is an alcoholic." I considered my words.

"It's not the same, but you, dear little eight-year-old girl, how can you be expected to know the difference?" I took the glass and the nearly full bottle, walked over to the sink, and poured them down the drain.

"Debi," I said, looking down at her young face, "never again will you see me drink any kind of alcohol." The promise was made for Debi's sake, but in the hard years that followed, it served me well.

My steps of faith were faltering. Growing in faith alone takes considerably longer than it would among other growing Christians. The negative circumstances of our daily lives were not conducive to good health or spiritual growth.

As I drew back to God, I increasingly felt the need to find a church. On occasion, Bill would agree with me about our need, and gradually we began to look for a church home. The criteria weren't complicated—evangelical, Bible-believing, concerned with mending broken lives. We needed to serve and be served. Corrected but not condemned. Did such a place exist?

Our felt need was for healing, honesty, and help. If we'd been able to give more, if we'd evidenced spiritual health and stability, perhaps we'd have been more readily received. But that would've forced us to live out another lie.

Our search resulted in visits to twenty churches in the Cajon Valley. Large, professional churches, too busy for people. Small, comfortable churches, too closed to outsiders. Sometimes we were the only ones who brought a Bible, and by the conclusion of the service we understood why—they weren't needed. Other times we were gladly considered as "space fillers" or "budget builders." In due season, we would give, but first we needed to know they cared enough to help us mend.

Perhaps we'd been expecting too much. We discontinued our search.

We pulled back into our own lives. One afternoon I watched an old movie on television as I ironed. Bill sat solemnly in the corner chair. When a voice interrupted the movie to rave on in superlatives about the merits of some detergent, I seized the opportunity to go out to the clothesline for the remainder of the laundry.

It seemed too quiet when I returned. The familiar heaviness found its place within me. Bill had sneaked out of the house and was gone. The television was gone. I felt more indignant about losing the TV in the middle of the movie than I did about losing it to a pawnshop. At least he could've waited until the movie was over. But drinking is costly. Its drives are strong. It seldom takes into consideration the wants or needs of others. I didn't feel like ironing.

Trite and nagging injustices were my destroyers. Little, seemingly insignificant things like an unfinished movie, a cherished coin taken from my collection, a lie uncovered, another broken promise. These daily disappointments tore away at my inner being. Light and lofty aspirations were crushed under reality's blows. Irretrievable years were lost forever in the pulls of another's indulgence. Aborted beginnings died and stockpiled like old cars in a junkyard.

All the while, Bill freely came and went as he pleased. Then one day he announced he'd gotten an apartment and planned to move out.

This news scared me into making an appointment with a legal aid lawyer to ask him if I should be considering a legal separation. After only a few minutes into our conversation, I felt so uncomfortable that I'd even considered taking such a step that I excused myself and left his office. I took Debi by the hand and returned home to our empty duplex feeling sad but convicted in the choice not to take any legal action.

Perhaps one of the more visual representations of our lives during this time was the property in Lakeside where we had had our trailer. This fertile soil, nurtured by the hand of God, had every potential to produce a rich, productive return. But tending it was essential. When we bought the property, it was covered in a lush green blanket of oats—healthy and growing. Now neglected, only dry stubble remained.

Massive amounts of prickly tumbleweeds blew in with a storm and idly lingered, making passage impossible. The corral sat empty. The garden had become parched and barren. Wild weeds choked the plant life. I identified.

Although our lives had become barren, I didn't forget my plea to God. We didn't attend church, but I clung to the basic principles of faith in as much as I was able. I hadn't made any life-style changes blatantly defying God. I still found it important to teach Debi what I knew of God and His truth.

It concerned me greatly to not live as I taught. I'd taken my short term in Bible college seriously. The learning broadened my understanding of how very short we fell as a Christian family. At times I strongly wished Bill wouldn't even make the claim of being a Christian. Then I wouldn't need to try to understand the constant contradictions or try to explain them to a child. I wondered if Debi would be able to erase this distorted view of Christianity from her mind. This concern kept rising.

Back in 1969, our initial encounter with Redwood Chapel Community Church in Castro Valley, some twenty miles east of San Francisco, was a pleasant one. We'd attended there just prior to leaving for Bible college, and now, as I pondered the concerns of our lives, this church came to mind. Perhaps a church so receptive six years ago would still welcome us now. And not only was this a friendly church, it also had a new Christian school. It would be costly to move again, but monies from the sale of the Lakeside property could make it possible.

"Debi, if I can just enroll you in a Christian school, then you will see how 'real' Christians live!" I told her. "And you can sing in the children's choir and go to Sunday school and make friends." The excitement we both had at the thought of such a possibility overrode the earlier news that Bill had somehow gotten himself an apartment and was going to leave us.

I continued teaching. The Cajon Valley school district obtained use of the Boy's Club building only two blocks from our duplex, so Debi and I went together to school without transportation. Taking Debi to work with me eliminated the need to put Debi in an after school day-care center. I was thankful to God for this provision because she thoroughly enjoyed the diversified intersession.

Bill was having difficulty paying for his apartment and extravagant life-style, so he came over to get a settlement from our Lakeside property. It was then that I decided to tell him of the plan Debi and I had been considering in the past month.

"Bill, I'd like to go back to the Bay Area to enroll Debi in Redwood Christian School," I said. "With my portion of the money, I'd appreciate it if you'd buy me a used car. I don't care what kind it is as long it doesn't have a clutch. Then, I wondered if you would consider driving the U-Haul truck up there for us, because I can't drive a truck. Once there, no expectation will be put on you. You can leave if you wish. All of the expenses can be deducted from my half of the money from the property."

He agreed. Then he went out and bought me a used sports car (with a clutch). We loaded the U-Haul and headed north. I'd hoped to live in Castro Valley, but the closest place we could afford was a duplex in nearby San Leandro. Once we had arrived in the Bay Area, Bill changed his mind about leaving us.

Debi and I had a Monday morning appointment with the headmaster of Redwood Christian School, followed by an appointment with the pastor of Redwood Chapel Community Church. Excitement welled up within me. The lace on Debi's freshly sewn dress encompassed her pretty face. Her long, blond braids fell softly to the bow at her waist. Her face shone with an inner beauty that bore witness to her sweet spirit. Debi and I hesitated at the front door to pray for new beginnings.

The appointment with the headmaster was brief. I was caught off guard, and it took a great deal of effort to hold my composure. Debi was denied entry. I was angry such a judgment could be placed so quickly and unemotionally. How could this man know the potential of this young life? How could he so matter-of-factly deny her entry? How could the school refuse to be a part of the molding and shaping of this pliable child? How much pain could our hearts withstand?

Fighting the swelling tears, I took Debi's hand and

walked away from the grey building toward the street where Bill sat waiting for us. Unable to control the tears, I decided it was futile to go to our next appointment with the pastor, so we drove on home. It took me three years to forgive that man.

We moved to south San Francisco in order to enroll Debi in another Christian school and attend another church. They hired me to teach, Debi enrolled, and Bill took on a job in the city. We should have been happy, but I was ill at ease about some of the things I was told to teach and, subsequently, about what Debi was learning.

God began to penetrate my protective shield. He caused me to realize we'd made a wrong move. It began to occur to me that His plans might be different from mine. Debi and I began an aggressive prayer campaign to find and follow God's will for our lives.

We wanted to go back to Redwood. We desperately wanted a home and stability. I wanted to find a home in Castro Valley and quite possibly never, ever move again. I wanted to walk the Christian walk with my daughter in a manner that had some respectability to it. Bill claimed the Lord's ownership, but his allegiance didn't verify his claim as he continued to give himself to sexual immorality. My broken spirit had neither power nor testimony. God alone should have been our source of stability, but I still relied upon Bill.

Slowly, Debi and I grew accustomed to depending

upon and consulting with God. In prayer we asked God, in explicit detail, to provide us with a home in Castro Valley. We asked that it be within walking distance of Redwood Chapel, the public school, and the grocery store. We asked for an affordable rental amount, a room and yard for Debi, and a neighborhood with some feeling of safety. For all of Bill's irresponsibility, he'd always come through with the rent, so I didn't feel we were amiss in our prayer, which Debi and I presented to God continuously for two months. Bill didn't join us in our prayer campaign and it took a lot of coaxing to get him to agree to drive us the forty minutes from south San Francisco to Castro Valley, but his disinterest changed when it appeared as though we'd found a place.

September 1, 1976, we moved into our lovely home in Castro Valley. Every facet of our prayer had been answered. Debi walked to Vannoy School on the first day of her fourth grade class. On Wednesday evening we walked together to enroll her in Pioneer Girls where I also became a Guide. Thursday afternoons she hurried home from school to make it in time for Sonshine Singers' Choir practice. Everything we needed was within walking distance. Fifty other families had applied for this home, but it was our prayer that was answered affirmatively. Debi and I thanked God daily for His kindness toward us, for His wonderful unmerited favor. Debi went on to attend Canyon Junior High and Castro Valley High. All three schools were within a mile radius of our home.

As the years passed, God continued to carry the burdens that threatened to weigh me down. Additionally, I was seeing Him as Provider and Comforter. Each dependent step reinforced His dependability. Each answered prayer strengthened my hope in Someone greater than my circumstance.

Bill constantly vacillated back and forth on his pendulum of good and evil. He got a job, then used his paycheck to nurture his sexual desires. He recognized that God had provided our home, then drove away from it to sleep in a sleazy hotel. He spent the evening reading the Word, then put it aside to ponder his own lustful thoughts. He consented to meet regularly with one of the pastors to study and to pray but disregarded his advice.

Meanwhile, Debi and I attended church as regularly as we could without causing further problems at home. Sometimes Bill would allow us to go, but the cost was high; he'd go into an angry rage, and I'd walk in the door to find him gone and my pearl necklace, my camera, and a dozen smashed eggs on the kitchen floor.

The more often I was around people, the more lonely I felt. Living in an upper-income community magnified our sense of poverty. Since that night out on the property, I realized how very fragile my mind's limits were; I realized we could only be pushed so far before breaking.

The longing for a person I could call my friend was deep and persistent. So I fervently prayed that

God would send a confidant willing to stand by me and uphold me in prayer. Ten years of carrying burdens, keeping secrets, and living a lie left me in need of such a friend to pull me out of the mire. If I had been more mature spiritually, I would have known how to allow God to fill this need. But He knew my limitation and was gracious.

Even after ten years, I hadn't told my family about Bill's excessive drinking or his homosexual involvements. Having my dad's respect and approval was of utmost importance to me. And except for Debi, my life was a failure, as far as I was concerned, so I just kept it all to myself. Every time Bill would show a renewed commitment to God, it confirmed my belief that it was best to keep our private lives private. Fear also controlled my decision to remain silent—fear that if I revealed Bill's life-style secrets, I might make it harder for him to forsake them and thereby add to his pattern of self-destruction.

One Saturday morning Jean Doty and I were praying together for the church, her husband's Sunday message, and our children. We'd been praying together regularly for several months before I realized she was God's answer to my prayer for companionship. What a friend she turned out to be! Like an angel of mercy, she saw me through the healing process. It took a long time to regain ground because Bill so constantly reopened the wounds.

Eventually, Bill agreed to come with Debi and me to Redwood. His passion for God would surface on those occasions when he estimated he'd sufficiently cleaned up his act. Pastor Williams and Pastor Doty were as supportive as he would allow them to be. When he did not want to attend church, we stayed home and watched Redwood's services on the cable station. At least now we were being ministered to, even if we couldn't always be in attendance.

As summer approached, I oftentimes volunteered to do various projects for Vacation Bible School. Debi invited all the girls in her fourth grade class to join her in different activities at the church. In September of 1977, I received a phone call from the church office. A part-time position was opening up in the graphics department, and I was being asked to come and fill in an application.

What a perfect opportunity, and what a privilege to be back in God's service. By the end of the first week I was convinced I'd never get that old offset printing press to cooperate with me, but somehow I conquered it. Even with the noise and fumes and ink under my fingernails, I had a sense of dignity that came from being in the place God had led me to.

God kept on blessing. Debi and I kept on growing. With a boldness once foreign to me, I stepped out from under Bill's authority whenever it contradicted God's edicts.

"Bill," I said, with a power boost from within, "don't ask me to call into work and tell them you have the flu when you have a hangover, because I won't do it any longer. Please don't ask me to write checks before the deposit, not even one day ahead. Because I won't do it. I won't lie, and I won't cheat people. I mean what I say. I don't mean to be unkind to you, but what I've been doing isn't doing either one of us any good, and it certainly doesn't honor God. Please try not to get angry. These words are not meant to hurt you. It's what I have to do."

He didn't like it at all, but he didn't fight it. He knew in his heart the difference between right and wrong. He was threatened by my new strength of character. Many times I was afraid when I stood up to him, but I had to. I voluntarily placed myself and Debi under the authority of the church. When a question arose, I would have someone who could be objective beyond Bill's legalisms give counsel.

My days of spiritual healing began that night in Lakeside when I poured out my broken heart to God. It was so good to walk in the protection of His care. *Perseverance* had become our key word—standing firm when it would've been so much easier to fall. Being upheld by my friendship with Jean and others from Redwood made a considerable difference.

We weren't walking alone anymore. Counsel was available whenever we asked. This is how God led us along.

GIVEN THE CHOICE

Eight

Over the next three years, the frequency with which Bill pursued his secret endeavors increased radically. Once a month became once a week, then twice and three times a week he'd be gone. Regularly. It wasn't uncommon for him to be gone through the night. Eventually a pattern began when he would leave all together. Then days, weeks, or months later, he'd return with his story of repentance. I'd accept him back. He would do well for a time. But the pattern would start all over again.

One evening in the summer of 1979, I stood by the front room window waiting for the last commuter bus of the day to come into view. Cresting the hill, it stopped and several weary-looking passengers stepped down and scattered like ants without their leader. The one person for whom my eyes searched did not appear. The bus continued down the hill to deliver the remaining suburban dwellers to their respective homes.

A passive, defeated attitude of "Who cares?" permeated my thoughts as I headed for the kitchen to take the dinner off the stove—again. Halfway across the room I stopped. *This marriage is a joke,* I thought. I recognized the danger of being resigned to passivity. *God must have something to say in the Bible about marriages that are a mockery,* I reasoned.

If we had been living in Old Testament times, I knew I wouldn't have to be figuring it out. I remembered reading in the book of Leviticus that it is forbidden for a man to lie with a man as one lies with a woman (Lev. 18:22). And if a man does lie with a man as one lies with a woman, he has done what is detestable. They were to be put to death, and their blood was on their own heads (Lev. 20:13).

But it's not the Old Testament times, I thought. *We are living under God's grace, as we've well experienced! But still,* I reasoned as I stood in the middle of the room, *He must have something to say about this issue today. He's the same God.*

That evening I began an extensive and intensive study in God's Word on every passage I could find addressing conditions of our marriage—perpetual adultery; homosexual behavior; and physical, emotional, spiritual, and financial abandonment. I also studied the nature of forgiveness, reconciliation, and legal responsibility as a believer. Night after night I took my Bible and reference books and studied alone. Later I would seek the counsel of my pastor, but I felt that I first needed to see for myself what the Scriptures said.

The first verses I studied were in the fifth chapter of Matthew. There in verse 27 I found God's command to not commit adultery. Verses 31 and 32 helped me to understand the grounds upon which a divorce could be obtained: "Anyone who divorces his wife, except for marital unfaithfulness, causes her to become an adulteress, and anyone who marries the divorced woman commits adultery." I read in Malachi 2:16, "'I hate divorce,' says the Lord God of Israel"; in Matthew 19:1-11, I saw that God permitted divorce because of the hardness of man's heart. Mark 10:1-10 gives the account of Jesus' response to the Pharisees as He reminded them—and me, "But at the beginning of creation God 'made them male and female' . . . and the two will become one flesh." God created not male and male or female and female but clearly male and female.

I continued referencing my concordance and paralleling versions until I had exhausted my resources. Then I studied the directives regarding taking another to court. Because Bill claimed to be a believer, I followed the pattern of Matthew 18:15-17, "If your brother sins against you, go and show him his fault, just between the two of you. If he listens to you, you have won your brother over. But if he will not listen, take one or two others along, so that 'every matter may be established by the testimony of two or three witnesses.' If he refuses to listen to them, tell it to the church; and if he refuses to listen even to the church, treat him as you would a pagan or a tax collector."

When I reached a point of conclusion, I made an appointment with our pastor to clarify with him what I understood the Bible to say. I told him I was intending to divorce Bill. However, if he estimated I was just tired of fighting to maintain a marriage that was a lie, tired of living with an alcoholic, tired of the degradation—or, if I had read the Bible to my own convenience or misinterpreted its meaning—I would not proceed. I asked the pastor to confirm or to reject my findings. I would abide by his counsel.

Giving my word to such a commitment was not done lightly. It wasn't an easy step to take. In 13½ years of pleading, praying, and despairing, I had always been very sure divorce was not an option. I had made a vow. I meant to keep it. Unfortunately, Bill never did. My pastor heard me through, then confirmed my right under God to divorce and to remarry.

I followed the process described in Matthew 18 that instructed me to first go to Bill privately to show him his faults. If he listened, I would have won him over. But he didn't listen.

The next step was to bring in witnesses. Jean and Neal joined me in confronting Bill. He acknowledged his guilt and asked our forgiveness, promising to stop going to bars and doing homosexual deeds. But the desire within him to continue the deeds would repeatedly build until he got in the car and drove off into the night. There were leavings and reconciliations but no lasting changes. My final great effort to pull our marriage together ended with a question.

"Bill," I asked, "if you had to make a choice between God's ordained plan for marriage or the homosexual life-style, which would you choose?"

"Given the choice," he responded, "I would choose the homosexual life-style."

My heart wrenched. To such a statement, I had no response. I knew what had to be done now. I asked Bill to sit down while I told him of my intent to divorce him because of his perpetual sexual sin and his subsequent rejection of Debi and of me. He did not say anything until I was done.

"I understand," he said quietly. "I don't know why you didn't do this years ago."

"Within myself I did not have the freedom to do so until now. I had always hoped you would choose to change," I responded.

The weeks before Bill's actual move were awkward and hard on each of us. I still wished Bill would change. I wondered how to tell Debi.

I felt it was so unjust—how one person's choices could have such an effect on the rest of the family. Taking Bill's clothes from the closet, I looked down at a pair of his shoes and wondered where they had walked—into bars, into bathhouses, and beside strange beds. I packed them away with his belongings.

I had given Bill the option of taking whatever possessions he wanted to take, so on August 25, 1980, he loaded our station wagon with all the things important to him. When it reached capacity, Bill came into the kitchen where Debi and I soberly waited.

"Well, I guess this is good-bye," he said. "Everything's in the car."

Neither Debi nor I knew what to say. With tears, we gave Bill a farewell hug. He turned, walked through the garage, and stepped into the car. His sad eyes looked back for a moment, and he awkwardly motioned a wave. Debi and I watched as he slowly drove down our street and disappeared from our sight. It was four years before we saw him again.

Returning to the house, my vision blurred with tears, I began packing for the week Debi and I were going to spend at Mt. Hermon Conference Center in the Santa Cruz Mountains. It sounded like a good idea when I first thought of it some weeks back, but now I wondered what we were doing going to a "family camp" with a fragmented family.

"Debi, please load your bag and put it in the car," I said. Busyness had always been my way of covering my feelings of despair.

Bill had taken our newer station wagon and left me with the old Bonneville. It was oversized, and I was afraid to drive it through the mountains. But if I was going to have to do it, I wanted to get it over with as quickly as I possibly could. Through all our years together, Bill had always insisted on doing the driving. Mt. Hermon was only an hour and fifteen minutes south, but I'd never driven that far. I pulled out of the driveway, resenting the responsibility. Seeing my anxiety, Debi sat quietly in the passenger seat.

I prayed my way through the traffic and down the freeway. When we reached the stretch of road entering the Santa Cruz Mountains with a bank on one side and a concrete divider on the other, I was convinced it would never accommodate this great hulk of white metal surrounding us. Reason told me to cling to the white line on my left and the rest of the car would have to make it. So I forged ahead—my hands glued to the wheel, my eyes to the road.

God's grace got us there. We said a prayer of thanks as we turned into the conference center. Dear friends permitted us the use of a floor of their old three-story cabin, lovingly named "Houseman's Hobby." It had been constructed at the turn of the century, and its floors sloped and creaked with the memory of so many guests walking in and finding solace. The conference grounds, tucked neatly into the redwoods, became, over a period of years, our healing place.

Each August Debi and I returned to the old cabin. We discovered our tearing wounds were deep and slow to heal. Sometimes I felt as if we'd made no progress at all. The part of me that had been severed the day Bill drove away took years to heal. My understanding of God's ability to look after us would be clear for a time, then fog over when I encountered a hardship.

I moved my wedding ring from my left hand to my right and yet wished that I was still a wife. I would dream of being happily married to Bill, then have nightmares about his rejection of me. The healing thoughts that I was able to allow God to control during the day were often undone by the horrid dreams of the night. But in due time my sleep became sweet and dreamless, and I knew God's grace was subduing the loneliness and sadness and slowly producing healing.

Along the way, we had stumbled into steps and stages of healing, countering society's "instant everything" mentality. The expectations of those who had not suffered the severance of a marriage continually posed a potential problem. Additionally, the expectations we placed on ourselves were, at times, unbelievably unrealistic. We couldn't deny that it was going to take time.

On the premise of logic, I believed healing would follow fast behind freedom. But legal and emotional bonds are loosed on separate timetables, and the one is not a guarantor of the other. The fact that a married couple becomes one flesh may be the cause for this. The courts can pronounce you free long before your heart does—even in a marriage as severely defiled as ours.

TEARING INEQUITIES

Nine

The day the divorce became final I felt a part of me was actually severed, like an arm torn from its socket. With a signature, and a flimsy two-dollar receipt, it was over—thirteen and a half years of marriage finished. Tears flowed from my broken heart for hours.

Whenever people would refer to our divorce as the beginning of our separation, I would silently recall the inequities that had ripped us apart long before the divorce papers. The first rip was the continuous rejection. Night after sleepless night, Bill would turn away from me; month after month, year after year, he had no desire for me. Stabbing deeper in later years was the knowledge that he gave himself in hundreds upon hundreds of immoral relationships. I couldn't win; I couldn't even compete.

The second rip in our relationship was the name. One day very soon after we were married, I discovered a driver's license lying on the floor of our clothes closet. Looking up to the shelf from which it had fallen, I found yet another license. Moderately curious, I studied Bill's photo on each one. They were the same. My eye moved to the statistics; they, too were the same. But now I saw something shocking: each license bore a different name. Different from each other, and different from Bill's present name.

Puzzled, I met Bill at the door when he came home from work. Before he secluded himself in his studio, I needed some answers.

"Bill, why do you have two other driver's licenses with different last names than your own? One even has another middle name. I don't understand. How can a person have three driver's licenses?" I asked. "Why do you have them, and whose names are they?"

"Where did you get those?" he asked, his facial expression a mixture of anger and guilt.

"In the closet. One was on the floor," I said.

"Well, I was going to tell you anyway," he said.

"Tell me what?" I asked.

"About the name," he said. "It's not my name."

"What's not your name?" I asked. I could feel my heartbeat accelerate, and I began to be afraid.

"The one in my wallet, and the one in your hand," he said as he pointed to one of the licenses I held.

"Bill, you are not making any sense. Your name is

William Ronald Bowerman. Whose names are these others? Who is William R. Brock? And who is William Hamilton Eby?" I asked.

"I am," he said. "I'm William Hamilton Eby. That is my real name."

"You can't be! It can't be! I married you—William Ronald Bowerman. What about our marriage certificate? I saw you sign it, and I saw you sign the application for our marriage license at the courthouse. Your name is Bowerman, William Ronald Bowerman." I repeated the words as if saying them would make them true. What did all this mean? What was this man hiding—and why? Were we ever legally married? I became even more frightened. To discover we were married under an assumed name was an unbelievable revelation.

Bill assured me that by virtue of usage, the name Bowerman was legal. I was too ignorant and confused to pursue the matter further. He also pointed out that changing our marriage records would cause undue hardship and a barrage of questions from the authorities. If I had been smarter or wiser, I would have continued with my own barrage of questions; I would have thought to ask him to prove his truthfulness to me. There was, however, one question that led to my next tearing discovery.

"Bill, tell me why you changed names," I said.

"It had to do with some money I owed. But that was a long time ago. It has nothing to do with now," he said.

"What name did you use when you were married before?" I asked.

"Eby," he said.

"Did you ever get a divorce?" I asked. I couldn't believe our whole line of conversation.

"She did."

"Are you sure?"

"Yes, I'm sure." I was not assured, but his tone told me he was done with my question.

What a fool I had been! But who would have thought that I needed to ask my husband if his name was real; if our marriage was legal; if he had any outstanding wives, debts, or bench warrants; or if he preferred to be intimate with men? Even when I did ask, I only was told what was already exposed. It wasn't until many years later that I learned he'd had not one, but three wives before me. And a child. I felt torn and doubly cheated by the revelations.

The next fracture came with his explanation of his paranoia about the police. His fears were well founded; I eventually discovered there was a warrant pending. It crossed my mind that I might be a candidate for deportation if I probed any deeper into Bill's chasm of secrets. When the qualifying day arrived to apply for citizenship, I was afraid to fill in the application because of Bill's false names, past debts, unpaid taxes, and undisclosed wives. I was too conscientious to lie, and too afraid to tell the truth. Only seven years after the divorce did I finally obtain U.S. citizenship.

The first time Bill stayed out all night, without a word or a clue as to his whereabouts, I was eight and a half months pregnant. I stood at the window from early evening until the rising of the sun. Busses, taxis, and hours went by, and I stood there, dumbfounded, forcing myself to stay calm, fearing I might go into labor. At 8:30 I finally called his boss to see if he'd gone to work. He hadn't. In desperation I told her he had not come home.

Around 10:00 A.M. Bill walked in, covering his tracks with practiced flair. He was angry to discover I had told his boss, and not long after that he was fired. Added to the unthinkable number of nights Bill was gone until morning were the times he would suddenly move out. I would come from work to find he wasn't there. Then I would begin to notice that appliances, pieces of jewelry, and other small furnishings were missing. I felt robbed as well as torn.

One day, while I was teaching school in El Cajon, my boss brought us home. As we pulled up alongside our trailer park, I hoped he wouldn't notice the truck pulling away in front of us.

"Isn't that your El Camino?" he asked.

"Yes," I said, downcast with embarrassment because he had correctly perceived that Bill was trying to sneak away unnoticed.

"Aren't those your things loaded in the back of it? Are you moving?"

"No. I . . . well, I'm not. . . ." My speech wandered off as I looked ahead at our stuff haphazardly piled in the bed of the truck. It was the sight of the iron that roused my indignant anger. It was bad enough to have my boss viewing this scene. But worse than that to me was Bill's audacity in taking my iron. He never ironed! I painstakingly pressed his every item of clothing. And now he was stealing my iron.

"Is there anything I can do to help?" my boss inquired, sympathetically summarizing the situation.

"No. Thank you. I just need to get in and explain things to Debi," I said as I helped her from the car. When Bill returned and put back what he still had of our stuff, I accepted and forgave. But the scar was still there.

As a result of the unpredictability around us, Debi carried her own set of emotional scars. She seldom received the comfort of having an acceptable reason for the things happening around her. I had a difficult time discerning what I should or should not tell her. Most of Bill's decisions were made independently of me or Debi, and so it was often long after the fact when we had to deal with things. That is how it was with the loss of Debi's horse.

Debi was over at the neighbors' watching them groom their prize-winning horses in preparation for an upcoming parade. The brushing, braiding, and trimming took a good part of the day, and Debi was fascinated. Meanwhile, I worked in our garden. Bill was off somewhere. A dirty old dented truck drove down our easement, and a man of characteristics similar to the truck got out at our trailer door.

Nervously clinging to my rake, I watched him start toward the corral.

"Can I help you with something?" I called out.

"I come ta look-it my horse," he yelled back.

Running to close the gap between us and at the same time maintaining a reasonable distance for safety, I challenged the rough-looking trespasser.

"But that's not your horse. He's ours."

"Look, lady, the horse is mine. I bought him last night at the bar, fair and square. Ask your old man. He sold him to me," he said, continuing in the direction of Beauty. "I got a guy whose gonna buy him, an' I wanna make sure your old man didn't cheat me. The horse's name is Beauty, right? And your old man's name is Bowerman, right? See this piece of paper here? This says the horse is mine."

I couldn't dispute the signature. I couldn't fathom the act. The gruesome character of a man left satisfied as though he could taste the profit of his barroom purchase. The next day a family came to take Beauty.

If there was to be any consolation in such a deed of tearing cruelty, it was in the knowledge that, in fact, the horse was now probably better off. I had seen Bill hold a lit cigarette within inches of Beauty's startled face, clinging to the railing in a drunken stupor. The people who took Beauty to a new home were respectable owners of several horses, and knew what they were buying. They were very much into the circuit of competition and wanted to use Beauty for show. For Debi I wept, but for the horse I was glad. Now Beauty could run and be free and realize his potential. He would escape the inflictions of an unkind master.

If there was any consolation in the tearing agony of divorce, it was in the knowledge that we, too, had been set free from the oppressive deeds of an immoral husband and an unfaithful father.

Sometimes I hear people flippantly say, "Well, you know it's a fifty-fifty proposition, and both parties are guilty in a divorce." Instead of cringing and dying inside, I quietly, strongly say, "No, that is not always the case." Perhaps the kindest thing Bill ever did for me was to tell our pastor he found no fault with me. He, who knew my inadequacies and all my shortcomings, found me blameless of cause—for his deeds, for the death of our marriage.

THE "REALLY" REASON

Ten

It was two full years after the divorce before Debi began to process her feelings, perhaps because I had so strongly reinforced the teaching of "hate the sin but love the sinner." Debi was instructed not to hate. I didn't degrade her dad when I was speaking to her. When he left, I taught her to forgive him for all his deeds of abandonment. And even though Debi recognized and agreed with this teaching, which was based on Matthew 6:14-15 ("For if you forgive men when they sin against you, your heavenly Father will also forgive you. But if you do not forgive men their sins, your Father will not forgive your sins."), she was only twelve years old. She had limited understanding and lifelong memories consisting of disappointment, fear, and heartbreak.

The time she sang her first solo, I watched her repeatedly scan the congregation in search of her dad. He didn't come. Even worse were the times he did show up at important events, arriving late, drunk, and impatient to return to his folly.

Debi remembered the day she came home from her friend's house to find that her beautiful pony was gone. She remembered our long walk in the heat when her little legs felt like crumbling and long rides on her bike when her dad had a taste for beer and made her follow him as he rode his ten-speed into town. She remembered in fear how he had followed her home from school in our green station wagon—two or maybe three blocks back. She thought he'd come to kidnap her. But when it came to the important things like banquets, sports events, or graduations, he offered regrets, apologies, and excuses. But never was he there.

Yet she was told to love him. Debi didn't know what to do with the feelings contradicting my instructions, so she bottled them up inside. Added to the pain and disappointments she felt as a child were the unknown revelations she would come to understand about her father. Knowing she was unaware of his sexual practices, I was forever faced with the question of timing and the fear of compounding. How do you tell a twelve-year-old girl that her father is a homosexual? When do you tell her? *Do* you tell her? What effect will it have on her in the long run? When can you begin to let the past slide away from the conversations of the present? Would it be better to say nothing—or would that be worse?

These are the questions I wrestled with. Not knowing the answers, I once again made an appointment with our pastor.

"Pastor," I said, "Debi's asking me why I'm divorcing her dad. Do I have to tell her about his homosexual behavior? I hadn't even told my lawyer until the very last appointment, and only then because I was concerned about custody. How do you tell a young girl that her father has sex with men? What will such news do to her?"

"You have to tell her the truth," he said, "because if you don't, she will one day find out and she will know you weren't honest with her. It will hinder her ability to believe you when you talk to her about the things of God. If you're not honest with her, she'll have no reason to believe you about anything. You must tell her the truth."

"But she's so young and so innocent. It doesn't seem fair to introduce her to such harsh realities," I protested in panic.

"Well, when you're ready," he said with understanding.

"All right, I promise I will," I told him as I left his office. In my heart I made an agreement with the Lord. I made a commitment to Him to tell Debi the truth about her father if she asked me. It was a big "if" because I never really thought it would occur to her to ask about a subject she knew nothing of.

Exactly two weeks later, Debi popped up on the kitchen counter, her special place to sit whenever she had something on her mind to talk over.

"Mom," she said, "what was the 'really reason' you divorced Dad? You told me he didn't have a new girlfriend, and you told me it wasn't because he drank so much and was gone so much. So, Mom, what was the 'really reason'?"

I could hardly believe it. She had asked me the question I promised to answer. She noticed the change in my composure as I tensed under the strain of the responsibility I now felt.

"It's OK, Mom. You don't have to tell me," she said.

"Oh yes, I do, Debi. I promised God and Pastor Doty I would. I do have to answer, but just give me a moment so I can tell you in the best way. Let's pray first and ask God to give me wisdom and sensitivity," I suggested.

Debi was only able to absorb little bits of information at a time. One of the more difficult elements of knowing the truth about someone is knowing what to do with the information you now possess. Over the next two years, Debi's indirect response to the news about her dad brought about disheartening changes in her choice of friends, her attitudes, and her behavior. Still she submitted, if only outwardly, to most of my disciplines.

Late in the summer, my brother sent me the airfare to attend a family reunion in Canada's

Yukon. At the same time Debi joined about eighty junior high kids from our church and headed south to Hume Lake Christian Camp, not far from Fresno. With 2500 miles between us, Debi was at last able to begin to express the deeply rooted feelings which had been building up within her to the point of danger. Her breaking point came as she listened to a group of her peers do a skit mocking "gays." She screamed out in hatred directed toward her dad. Her trauma sent her into a series of fainting spells which I later discovered were actually a succession of seizures.

This public outburst was the beginning of her admission that she hated what her dad was. She hated the pain, the humiliation, and the ridicule. She hated not having a dad when she needed him. She hated being told to love when she knew she hated.

When she returned from camp, I noticed disturbing signs of rebellion. Jean and I prayed fervently. I really thought I would die of a broken heart if I lost Debi to the grips of the world. Again, I sought counsel from our pastor and we prayed Debi would not involve herself in anything with long-range consequences. We talked and confronted issues together. As confused and angry as Debi was, it was never her intent to hurt me.

God held on to Debi, and the next summer at the same camp, through the ministry of one of their dynamic youth speakers, Debi rededicated her whole self to becoming a "bondslave of Jesus." She grew in her faith and faithfulness. She listened to the counsel given. She softened her heart. She involved herself wholeheartedly in the youth activities of our church. And, as the need arose, she responded cautiously but favorably toward her dad.

Perhaps if I'd ever seen anyone having a seizure, I would have recognized that the loss of consciousness, accompanied by stiff and contorted movements, was more than a fainting spell. Over the next three years, I became aware that when Debi was under emotional or medical stress, she was likely to pass out. On four separate occasions, this had happened while we were in the dentist or doctor's office. Shortly after having a blood test at a local hospital, Debi lost consciousness in the waiting room. Securing no assistance, I took care of her needs to the best of my ability. That evening I took out our home medical book, found her symptoms, and made my own diagnosis. I then documented the circumstances surrounding each fainting and discovered a strong link to emotional crises relating to Bill.

I closed the medical book and called her doctor, describing to him what he confirmed was a grand mal seizure. He prescribed a daily medication, which she adapted to very easily. Being sixteen, she had more trouble adapting to the fact that she now had to wait a whole year before she could apply for her driver's license. Only as I listened to the doctor's report and saw the documented relationship to our traumatic past did I have a clear picture of how very deeply the wounds had cut into Debi's emotional being.

My deepest prayer during the difficult years of recovery involved the matter of bitterness. I truly believed there is nothing worse than a person whose insides are eaten up with bitterness. I knew I had the potential to become bitter, and with every fiber of my being, I fought hard not to be. This was especially my cry when I considered what Bill's choices had done to our precious young girl. Over and over again I would pray, "Dear Lord, please help me not to be bitter."

I also prayed that God would help me go through the hard things with honor. I didn't want to disgrace His name, or the name Christian—"Christ's one." I prayed that when I was on the other side of all this trouble, I'd be able to look back without being ashamed of my own responses. I asked God for an extra measure of grace. And He gave it.

HEALING *Eleven*

God gave His grace to me and to Debi. He wanted to give it to Bill, but Bill rejected it. At some odd hour of the night, the phone would ring. It would be Bill calling from some bar in Los Angeles or San Diego or wherever he happened to be in his perpetual wanderings. Months, even years, would pass before we'd hear from him again. We seldom knew how to respond to him. Our feelings of hurt and anger were gradually subsiding, but it always set me back emotionally after I talked to him on the phone.

We sympathized with his myriad of problems, but until he was ready to take some initiative to receive help, there wasn't much we could do. When I couldn't pray for him because I simply didn't want to think of him, I asked a dear, elderly prayer warrior to pray for him on my behalf. Oftentimes when she couldn't sleep at night, she would lie awake and pray. I believe that until the day she went home to be with her precious Lord, she continued to bring Bill's name to the feet of Jesus.

With the breakup of our home, Debi and I were confronted by a variety of challenges, most of which we would rather have done without. Even though the court ruled Bill was liable for the debts he'd incurred, it would take a lawsuit to enforce the ruling. When a creditor wanted to collect, I was the one that could always be found. I was the one to be pressured. Whenever the phone would ring, I hesitated and asked God to go before me.

We made our way up from financial bondage. Creditors permitted me to send small payments. I earned a little too much to qualify for any assistance programs. But a real-estate broker engaged me to do free-lance artwork after my regular job. He appreciated my work and my self-esteem began to grow.

Bill never did send any money, but I hadn't expected him to. If he wasn't going to look after us before, it didn't seem likely he would suddenly begin now.

So, we scrimped along. Sometimes we had porridge for dinner. But we never were completely without. We thanked God we didn't have to move from the home which He'd so abundantly provided. We took special care in spending what we did have. In the winter, we bundled up and thanked God for a moderate climate. Often, when our need was greatest, someone from the church would arrive at our door with bags full of groceries.

Our pastor's family became our dearest friends. Jean's strong love for the traditions that build memories influenced us to make a special effort to celebrate holidays and vacations with a predictability that would ultimately add stability. The first Christmas was the hardest. But we forced ourselves to bring out the decorations, buy a little tree, and begin our own traditions. The tendency to want to postpone celebrations until things got better or until someone came into our life to make happy memories for us had to be pushed out of our thoughts. Debi's teen years could never be retraced. It was essential to live in the present, even when we didn't feel like it. We had to keep working at *enjoying* ourselves as a fragmented family until our deliberate efforts became *enjoyable* traditions.

So every year we bought our little tree at the same location on the tenth of December. We opened one gift on Christmas Eve, and we spent Christmas Day with our pastor's family. Every Mother's Day I was served breakfast in bed. And we saved all year for our summer vacation at Mt. Hermon and, in later years, Canada. We also established a pattern of routine medical and dental checkups.

Over the years we reestablished a respectable level of financial freedom. It took seven years before I could apply for a credit card and get one. Financial integrity was more the issue than the ability to "buy now, pay later." Now, on occasion, we even had the privilege of sharing in the financial needs of others.

Reaching out to the needs of others proved to be an essential element in the healing process. Taking our eyes from our own oppression to the felt need of a hurting friend or acquaintance accomplished therapeutic results for all parties involved.

During the week I gradually learned to live with being a divorced single. But on Sundays I remained vulnerable. My aloneness intensified as I entered church, often a couples-oriented setting. It occurred to me that other singles might feel this same sense of alienation. So I made myself available to meet and sit with other women who came alone. In due course we organized regular singles' Sunday school classes. Under the leadership of one of our pastors, we met for Bible study and conversation in my home. Many hours were spent relating God's love. We eventually outgrew our home and continued to meet at the church. Recreational fun added laughter and helped create a wholesome environment for parents and their children.

Debi preferred to join her youth group instead of the singles' activities because it made less of a point that she was from a single-parent home. When she did come to the outings, it was more for my sake than her own. Her interest in sports kept her attention when she did visit.

In time I, too, became involved in other areas of ministry. I redirected the thrust of my attention away from singleness to other activities in the mainstream of the church. For a number of years, I worked with international students and also a women's Bible study in my home in line with our church's commitment to small groups. Together the women of the Bible study and I delved into the Word to learn the fundamentals of becoming godly women. Some of the dear ladies were living examples of our lessons, and I felt terribly inadequate to presume to be their teacher. So we simply learned and prayed together, gleaning wisdom from the treasure of God's Word.

MY LOVE
JOURNAL

Twelve

The first time I noticed Peter, he was sitting across the room of our Sunday school class, alone. I wasn't the only one to observe him. My friend Linda had also taken mental notes. The next time I saw him, it was obvious he had already become acquainted with Linda. Over the following months they were often seen together, and I only knew him as Linda's special friend. By the time they announced their engagement, I felt Linda was getting a pretty terrific guy, and I truly wished her well. I had often wondered what it might be like to be married to a man with stability and success. I wondered if I would ever experience a true love relationship and marriage, as Linda was about to do.

For several weeks Linda's conversation pivoted

around her upcoming plans. Then, without warning, I noticed the absence of her beautiful diamond ring. Her countenance had changed. She seemed closed to any reference to Peter, so I withdrew from pressing her with questions. I stood by and waited until she was ready. In due time, she told me she'd called off the wedding. We really never did discuss the reasons. It was her choice, and before long she was seen in the company of someone new.

When Peter stopped me one Sunday after the evening service and asked if I'd like to go out for a cup of coffee, I responded more out of sympathy for him than profit for me. He looked so forlorn and in need of a friend. I agreed to accompany him to a nearby coffee shop and listened while he told of the heartbreak he'd gone through.

We talked with a comfortable ease. I could feel my attraction to him even though I was earnestly endeavoring to be no more than a friend to someone in need. Hour after hour, refill after refill, we were unaware of anything around us. It had been so many, many years since I'd felt drawn the way I was drawn to this man across the table. Suddenly, I was self-conscious, as though I had no right to think such thoughts.

When the phone rang the next evening, the sound of Peter's voice sent a surge of excitement through me. We talked for a long time. On Tuesday, he called again, and on Friday we attended a Good Friday supper together. I was so delighted to be with him. I wondered if he noticed Linda and her escort enter the room. If he did, it was not apparent. He extended his full attention in my direction.

As Linda was a friend, I was unsure if it was appropriate for me to be spending time with Peter. Even though she had assured me her relationship with Peter was over, I wanted to be careful not to do anything that would hurt her. While I was asking our pastor and his wife about this concern, Peter had gone to one of our other pastors to discuss the same question. Everyone concluded it would not be inappropriate for me to date him, so we pursued our new relationship with a sense of freedom.

Peter made plans to come over on Saturday to help me with some of the chores. When he arrived with two rakes in hand, I couldn't believe he was actually there, ready to do my yard! I felt like a giddy schoolgirl reeling from the effects of infatuation. It embarrassed and enthralled me at the same time. I just couldn't comprehend why this man, sophisticated and debonair, dressed in his designer clothes, would want to rake up leaves in my backyard. But there he was, and I was glad it was so. As the sun began its descent, we packed up the tools and headed out to nearby Pleasanton for a casual dinner and a relaxed evening of conversation.

We spent more and more time together. We attended church together. On the spur of the moment, Peter would invite Debi and me to join him for dinner or a day trip. He was generous to both of us. He secured a gardening service for us so we could have more free time to enjoy ourselves. He convinced Debi to resign one of her part-time jobs, then banked the equivalent monies into her college account. (He'd offered to have her discontinue both jobs to allow her more time for high school activities, but Debi declined his offer. She was committed to contributing to her future by the work of her own hand. I was proud of her decision.) Peter also invited us to join him at the gym a few mornings a week, then he purchased an annual membership there for each of us.

So many changes were taking place so rapidly. Sometimes Debi felt threatened. She had no real memory of sharing me with anyone. Even when she was a child, we spent the greater part of our time alone together. Peter included her, often, but she still had to struggle her way through the changes.

It was a new mix for Debi. She supported and encouraged me vigorously, but she had certain reservations and reactions to deal with as well. She worked hard not to allow her intuitive misgivings to dampen my spirit. Seeing me happy was an integral part of her orientation, even when it infringed on her sense of security.

I, on the other hand, knew I was beginning to fall in love. I was impossible at work—always off in a dream somewhere. My friends were glad to see me experiencing such happiness.

Desperately, I sought to hold my heart back, but to

no avail. It scared me to take a risk. At last, my world had become safe. Now I chanced being hurt again. Could I stand up under the disappointment if this dream came to an abrupt end? Could it be true at long, long last that I was going to experience a reciprocal love? Fear crept in and immobilized my thinking—but only momentarily. Then I was off in the whirlwind of dreamy bliss once again.

When Peter announced his growing attraction toward me, my fears melted into hopes. It was too good to be true. The days ahead were filled with surprises. Peter handed me a check for a thousand dollars and sent me off on a shopping spree. His only stipulation was to spend the money entirely on myself, in any way I chose, enabling me to feel comfortable to accompany him wherever we might go together. Never before had I known such an experience. Years and years of barely making ends meet left little for anything outside the essentials. My first inclination was to spend conservatively and save the balance. I knew, however, that was not the intent of the giver. He meant for me to receive his gift and to spend it.

Jeanie met me at the house, and we set off for Macy's with a "shop till we drop" mentality. Dresses, shoes, handbags, and accessories. Nails, hair, makeup—the works. When I stepped into his Mercedes that evening, I felt like a princess in a dream. We dined in a setting of meticulous elegance at the top of the Bank of America building in San Francisco.

Our window table overlooked the city which was adorned in a multitude of lights. Waiters stood in the recesses, ready to serve at the slightest hint. Peter spoke in soft, gentle tones. I soaked in the luxury and marveled to think people lived their lives this way.

Peter took it all in stride. He was amused by my pleasure in things so commonplace to him. Everything was perfect. The setting was soft and romantic. I adored the man sitting next to me. His desire and ability to care for me with eloquence far surpassed my greatest wish. The rich fragrance of his cologne hung on the air. The texture of his fine wool jacket gratified my sense of touch. His soft, penetrating eyes melted me to a pliable mass of vulnerability. My heart ached. I couldn't be more alive or more captivated. When the evening came to a close, Peter said good night at my door, then phoned the moment he arrived home. Sleep eluded me.

Throughout the week Peter either called or came over to visit. We were sitting in the front room looking through my Canadian photos the first time he kissed and tenderly embraced me. What a pleasure it was to be held by him. All those years of rejection, of crying out to God in my great need to be loved, were slipping out of sight. The love-starved years had come to an end. I was so very thankful.

As we progressed from the status of friendship to relationship, it became apparent we'd need to talk about the boundaries of intimacy. We openly discussed our potential to fail God and ourselves in a moment of careless abandon. My firm conviction that intimacy belongs within the confines of marriage had never before been put to the test. For the first time since becoming a Christian some nineteen years ago, I wondered about my capacity to violate my own convictions. I wondered how much I would allow the years of emptiness to control my logic and behavior now. Would compromise stain the pages of this love story as it entered a new chapter?

Peter had spoken of his love for me, and on occasion, he even spoke of marriage. He agreed with me in the desire to honor God as we faced these new temptations of intimacy. I decided, therefore, to put the responsibility on Peter to maintain the standard we had jointly set for ourselves. The fact that Debi was leaving shortly for a week in Hawaii heightened my concern for my own accountability. I was relieved to have discussed the issues with Peter, lessening the chances of failure.

The weekend Debi left for Hawaii exceeded my wildest expectations. Saturday was a clear, spring day with just the right amount of sun to draw sweet fresh scents from the variety of brightly colored flowers randomly arrayed on the hills surrounding us. We bid Debi and her girlfriend farewell at the airport and set out for a day of fun and adventure. In the evening we dined in romantic elegance at Halfmoon Bay's oceanfront Mira Mar Inn. After dinner we strolled and embraced as the breakers crashed and scurried up onto the sand, only to be absorbed back into the sea. Peter offered me his coat for warmth against the chill of the night air. I felt protected and secure.

The next morning Peter arrived in time to accompany me to the early worship service. We had planned to stop after church for breakfast at a local restaurant, but as we left Peter asked if I'd mind going out of the area for something to eat. He was concerned about bumping into Linda. He'd had her on his mind and wanted to avoid any confrontation. It wasn't so easy any more to have him thinking of her so constantly. But that was the premise upon which our friendship began. I had promised to allow him to heal in his own time and in his own way. It was a beautiful Sunday morning, and I was in favor of going anywhere he wanted to go.

We drove south on Interstate 880, stopping at the Hyatt Regency in San Jose for a poolside buffet. We then continued down the coast to the famed 17-Mile Drive. As we approached Pebble Beach, we decided to walk along the path at the edge of the golf course for a while before making our way back to Carmel. Peter made reservations for dinner at The Highland's Inn. We spent the latter part of the afternoon leisurely wandering through the quaint little shops of Carmel.

After having dinner the evening before at Half Moon Bay, then breakfast at the Hyatt, I hardly expected to be dining this evening at yet another place of such classic elegance. Walking at Peter's side, watching the valet drive off with the car, I was glad for the new outfit I had chosen to wear.

We took our place at a table for two, sipping Perrier water as we acclimated ourselves to the surroundings. I was totally encompassed. Behind me came the sounds of a master's hand at the keyboard. Below me the waves ravished the ragged cliffs. The air around me was heavy with the aroma of culinary excellence. And before me was the devoted attention of the man I was giving my heart to. I was flattered when Peter selected my favorite dish from the menu and ordered it for me. He made a point of never undermining my lack of finesse. He found a way to gently explain the peculiarities of upper-class etiquette, emanating an air of nobility without arrogance. Again, I felt protected.

After dinner we sat by the fire, receiving pleasure from the soft music and each other. Peter was a romantic through and through. And I loved him. As the evening progressed, I knew it was going to be a struggle to hold true to our commitment. The long drive home, his tight embrace, the yearnings from within. It would have been so easy to completely rationalize away reason and commitment. But, by the grace of God, we did not.

In the days ahead we were busy with our jobs, early morning trips to the gym, and untold hours on the telephone. Our conversation often centered on Linda, but more often we spoke of our own relationship and the direction it was taking. One day, to my astonishment and delight, Peter spoke of the honeymoon spot in the Canadian Rockies that would be his ideal: Jasper.

At the age of sixteen, I had worked six days a week folding sheets in the laundry room at Jasper Park Lodge. It was a hot, labor-intensive job. In the cool of the summer evenings, my workmates and I would sit in the shadows of the trees and watch the celebrities arrive. Waiters, dressed in formal attire, bicycled to the hide-away cabins, balancing silver-clad dinner trays on the tips of their fingers high above their heads.

Private visions of returning to Jasper someday, not as a laundry worker in a white uniform but as a registered guest, smartly clothed and on the arm of my own special someone, were formed that summer under the trees. So, of all the places in the world Peter could have thought of for a honeymoon, I was utterly amazed that he chose Jasper. I had loved the beauty of the lodge, set amid the ragged mountains and crystal clear waterways. It thrilled me to think we shared the same appreciations.

Debi and I were busy making plans to join our friends, Ralph and Leslie Ivey, for a weekend at Mount Hermon. Peter had met the Iveys some weeks earlier and we anticipated doing things in a foursome whenever our schedules for free time corresponded. Peter had a company party to attend but planned to join us at Mount Hermon on Saturday.

Prior to leaving for Mount Hermon, I observed a

difference in Peter's manner. He was cool and even abrupt. Suddenly he wasn't sure if he'd make it down on Saturday or not. He did not commit to a specific time. It didn't appear as though he'd be coming. It did appear as though all was done and over with. A picture of gloom formed in my mind. I tried to convince myself this was an acute case of overreacting. Inside me, however, I knew something had changed. My best efforts to present a cheerful front to my friends didn't fool them. They did their best to present a positive outlook.

Early Saturday I put on the coffee and purposefully prepared for Peter's questionable arrival. The morning fog left a heavy residue of mist on the weighty branches of the towering redwoods. The silence was only occasionally interrupted by an aggressive blue jay sending messages off into the woods. I walked along the path toward the road, determined to believe Peter would come. For an hour I watched and I listened and I chided myself for not being more aloof, feeling that if I had any sense at all, I should be back in the warmth and comfort of the cabin. Turning to make my way back, I suddenly stopped at the familiar sound of his approaching car.

Instead of going back to the cabin, we followed the path to the swinging bridge, walking and talking together as though all was well. Peter embraced me by the waterfall, and I did my best to cover the apprehension enveloping me. He spoke words of assurance. Because of my love for this beautiful place and my love for Peter, I pushed my doubts aside and set my mind on having a good and memorable day.

Ralph and Leslie left in the afternoon, and Debi and Peter played table games while I looked on. It did my heart good to see Debi and Peter getting along so nicely. On occasion, doubts would slip into my mind. Was the coolness in his voice evidence of a change of heart? Was his reluctance to commit to coming due to his schedule or to a lack of interest? Then we'd laugh and talk, and I'd release them.

Peter was ready to leave much sooner than I'd anticipated. He did not view this beautiful place from the same perspective as we did. But then, we had healed here. These grounds held memories Peter knew nothing of. The old cabin we loved so dearly was to him only an old cabin. My treasures fell into a different value system than his.

The discovery was a disappointment to me. We drove back together to the valley without much conversation. It was early in the evening when we arrived at my house, but Peter left immediately. He didn't call for the rest of the week.

At some point in our deepening relationship, Peter had begun to seek the advice of a counselor. The evening before I was to leave for a weekend retreat with the ladies of our church, Peter called to say his counselor had advised him to not see me for six months. He'd decided to follow her advice. He told me he didn't know why he felt so compelled to disconnect from me because I was everything he ever wanted. But he was going to disconnect. My heart broke at the words. He left our church, he walked out of my life, and I never saw Peter again.

No matter how familiar pain is, it hurts intensely each time you encounter it. In contrast to my feelings, I did have a quiet peace in my spirit that assured me God would sustain me. But I still hurt. The wonder of the past six weeks that had whirled in and just as quickly ripped away left me in a broken daze.

But in the midst of my suffering the great mercy of God allowed me a glimpse of understanding. For six magnificent weeks I had focused entirely on Peter to the detriment of my relationship with God. Not that I couldn't love God and Peter, too. But I'd been given very sound advice with regard to balances, and a red flag of imbalance had been waving. The rose-colored clouds were replaced with stark red reality. I pleaded with God to help me refocus.

Once I had asked Pastor Williams what quality a woman should look for in a man. Often enough I'd heard of the tendency to remarry a man of similar character to the initial choice. Although I didn't have any statistical proof for such tendencies, I did not want to fall victim a second time. Pastor Williams pointed out the wisdom of looking for a man who is prone to enhance your God-given abilities—one who takes time to discover what special tasks and gifts God has given, and then comes alongside to assist you to carry them out.

I knew Peter didn't find value in the task I was doing in meeting the graphics needs of Redwood Chapel. He felt I had a much higher earning power and should look for a more lucrative position outside the church. He didn't recognize the importance of ministry for me over and above the ratios of profit and loss. At first I thought that the concept of serving God in this way was just new to him. But his frame of reference and background differed so radically from mine that our views remained at a distance. It would be difficult for him to value and support what I'd dedicated myself to doing.

As I asked God to allow me to see Peter from a truer perspective than the dictates of my heart, I remembered Pastor William's words, and it made it easier for me to accept Peter's withdrawal from me. I still didn't understand why I couldn't experience lasting love. Jean told me that in time I would look back and thank God. I didn't believe I ever would. The fear of becoming bitter needed to be faced and dealt with—again.

The entries in the love journal I'd begun when I met Peter ceased. I stopped crying. My wound healed at the hand of the Physician. Once in awhile someone will pass by me wearing his cologne and my heart will twinge. I'll think of Peter for a brief moment, but then I'll move on. I liked the nice things Peter offered me, but the purposes of God give me more fulfillment in the long run.

It humbles me to realize the depth of God's love for me. I truly believe it was God's intervention that caused Peter to draw away, which leads me to conclude that Peter was not God's choice for me. And today, even though I am alone, I am confident that God is watching over me, and I do thank Him.

FIRST REUNION

Thirteen

Debi tried to cover her increasing tension as we drove toward the Greyhound bus depot. It was located only ten minutes from the house, but we left just after seven-thirty in case Bill's bus came in before the scheduled 8:10 A.M. arrival.

Debi hadn't seen Bill since that August morning four years ago. She'd grown from a child to a beautiful high school senior. Her emotions whirled, and she fidgeted nervously as we sat in our car, waiting for the bus to come into view.

For a moment my mind went back to other busses and other waits. I pushed away the thoughts. After all, it was Bill who had asked to come, and there wasn't any reason for him not to be on this bus. I forced myself to engage in lighthearted small talk with Debi to control my mood, but it took too much effort, so we sat silently.

"There it is, Debi," I said, as the large bus towered over the oncoming traffic. "Are you OK, sweetie?" I asked. I hated to see her so apprehensive.

"Yes, I guess so," she responded in a voice that really said she wasn't.

"Try to relax," I said. "We need to make Dad feel welcome, but just be yourself. Do you want to walk over to the place where he'll get off? I can't see into those dark windows."

"OK," she said and followed behind me. We watched the few tired-looking passengers step down from the bus.

"Mom, I don't think he's coming," Debi said.

"Wait a moment, Debi. Maybe he had to get his things from the shelf."

"No, Mom. All the passengers are off. He's not coming." I noticed a sick look of disappointment cross her face.

"Maybe there's another bus coming in from L.A. Come on, let's go to the desk and ask." My heart sank. The all-familiar feeling of years past swept over me. I fought it and went to the agent's desk to inquire.

"Yes, there's another bus coming via Fresno," the young agent replied. "It's due in at 9:00 A.M."

"See, Debi, I thought so," I said, with a confidence I didn't feel. It just wasn't conceivable to me Bill would betray Debi in this way. When he asked if he could come, we'd chosen to take him at his word. I prayed he wouldn't break it.

The nine o'clock bus came and went. Bill wasn't on it. I felt terrible for what I'd allowed him to put Debi through. Neither of us talked as we drove back to the house. I decided to call Bill to find out why he'd failed to keep his word.

"Hello, Bill. This is Sheila. Why are you still in L.A.? Why didn't you come? Do you have any idea what Debi has experienced today?" I asked. "I'm very sorry," he replied. "When it came time to get on the bus, I simply talked myself out of it. I couldn't believe you and Debi wanted to see me, so I turned around and went home. I'm sorry I let you down."

"Bill, we'll share the cost with you if you'll call the airlines and see if there's a flight into Oakland with available space. If we didn't want you to come, we would've said so. It's been four years since Debi has seen you. Please don't let her down."

Bill called back to let us know he'd booked a flight and would come into Oakland Airport shortly after five. If we reminded ourselves we were doing this more for him than for ourselves, it would be a little easier to take if he didn't show up. Yet it still was hard for Debi to separate her feelings and approach the day objectively. And I certainly could understand. No matter what his offenses, this man was still her father.

We arrived at the airport early. I usually found airports to be exciting hubs of activity. It was intriguing to imagine where people were going or where they were coming from. But today I was neither amused nor intrigued. I was extremely ill at ease and anxious to know if the hurrying group of arrivals would include Bill. *How many disappointments can Debi withstand,* I wondered, *without becoming embittered?*

In an almost unconscious effort to avoid further pain, we stood at the back of the crowd of greeters as the stream of passengers appeared at the far end of the ramp. The entire group dispersed, but there was no familiar face for us. We turned to leave when the corner of my eye caught the movement of a wheelchair on the ramp. Behind the large man pushing the wheelchair, was a much smaller man, one we recognized. It was, at last, Bill.

It was a new experience for Debi. The last twelve hours had been so full of ups and downs. And now she stood face-to-face with a man she hardly knew.

It was new for Bill because this tall, beautiful young lady standing before him was the child whose heart he'd broken. He wasn't accustomed to relating to a teenager, and Debi was no longer the little girl he remembered.

And it was new for me. I stayed back a bit to permit space for father and daughter to reacquaint themselves. Debi greeted Bill with a warm hug of acceptance. They both had tears in their eyes as they walked toward me.

We decided to drive into the city, to ride the cable car, to see the sights of Fisherman's Wharf and the shops of Pier 39. It seemed like a relaxed, unthreatening way to bring one another up to date. Bill responded well as Debi did an admirable job of making him feel comfortable and important to her.

The next day we all went roller-skating. As a young man, Bill had excelled at skating, so Debi decided they'd both have a good time. It was a church skating event, so Debi introduced her dad to all her friends. She was so proud to be able to announce she had a dad. And even though I stayed in the background, it did my heart good to see them laughing and having fun together. Debi showed no trace of the anger she had once felt, and as I looked inwardly, I found that my own sense of hurt had, with time, also subsided.

On Sunday, as we sat near the front of the church, I could see the tears of joy on the face of a friend as she looked out from her place in the choir. So many had prayed for Bill for so long. I prepared a special turkey dinner with all the trimmings. In the afternoon we took pictures in the yard and talked about Bill's desire to come up and live nearer to us.

In a few days we said good-bye with the promise that Bill would be back by Christmas. He claimed he wanted to make up for lost time and involve himself in being a father to Debi. But, Christmas came and there was no word from Bill. Debi busied herself with the activities of her senior year. She was an enthusiastic sports fan. And she'd been nominated for homecoming queen. She loved to go to all the football games and was always doing something with the high school group at church.

Before we knew it, it was time for graduation. We had a party and invited all the friends who'd shared a part in Debi's life and nurturing through the years without a dad. I cried as she joined the procession of graduates. Bill sent roses and his regrets.

As I captured Debi on film with my long-range lens, I pitied Bill for the great price he was willing to pay for his way of life. It was far from an equitable exchange. I concluded he'd been robbed far beyond his estimate of the cost. But this was Debi's night, and I refused to let thoughts of him cloud this glorious celebration.

DEBI, YOUR DAD HAS AIDS!

Fourteen

Mondays in the office were usually quiet. I was now responsible for the graphics department at Redwood Chapel. It was easy for me to become completely absorbed in the projects on my light table. Pasting up one, thinking ahead to another. My hand responded automatically in response to the ringing phone.

"Yes, this is Sheila," I said as I attempted to paste down a loose piece of copy. Transferring my attention to the phone, I noticed the line sounded like a long distance call. The voice of the caller could barely be heard.

"Hi, this is Bill."

"Hi, Bill, are you OK? I'm surprised to hear from you," I said.

"Sheila, I have something awful to tell you. You know I recently admitted myself into a detoxification program," he said.

"Yes," I answered, wondering what he was leading up to.

"Well, the doctor began with a routine examination. Then, without a word or a warning, they shuffled me all the way over to another hospital. I was terrified. They took one test after another. I think the doctors should've told me what they were doing. When I began the detoxification program, I didn't think they needed to know about the homosexuality, but I got so scared about what they were finding in their examinations that I decided to tell them the truth. They, in turn, told me nothing except to wait for the reports and cultures to return from the lab.

"Well, Sheila, I went back to the doctor this morning. He told me he had all the test results back from the lab. You know I told you recently that I was worried that I might have gotten the virus from someone? Well, the tests confirmed that I've gone beyond being a carrier of the virus. Sheila, I have full-blown AIDS—I'm going to die!" he said.

The words had tumbled out too quickly for my brain to assimilate and respond. I paused for a moment to digest what had been said.

"Bill, are you sure? How does the doctor know? What are your symptoms?" I asked. I searched for meaningful words of comfort. "I'm terribly sorry, Bill. Is there anything specific I can do for you? May

I call you back tonight when we can talk a little longer?" I asked.

"Thank you. I'd like that," he said and placed down the receiver. Putting down the receiver myself, I sat dazed by this sad news. It was not as though I hadn't realized the potential for this diagnosis. But I still found myself stunned by the reality that it had actually happened. Bill had AIDS.

Over the next couple of days, I had to decide how I would tell Debi. She had just returned to college in Portland, Oregon. I planned to go up there for Parents' Weekend in February, but I was afraid the word might get to her through someone else if I waited that long. So many of our church families interconnected with the school, and it would hurt her more to hear it from someone other than me. With these thoughts in mind, I decided it would be best to call. I'd wait until late Sunday evening to allow for a little more privacy as her phone was located in the dorm hallway.

I asked the Lord to go before me, to give me just the right words to break the news to Debi. I had no way of knowing how she'd respond, and although her Dilantin had kept her from having any more seizures, she had not faced quite as severe a test before. After I prayed, I picked up the phone to dial her number.

"Hello?" Debi answered.

"Hi Deb, this is Mom."

"Oh, hi, Mom. What's happenin'?"

Before I answered I had to find out if she was sitting or standing and if she was somewhat alone.

"Debi, when I call you at school, where's the phone?" I asked. "Do you have to stand in the hall and talk?"

"Yeah, the phone's in the hall. I'm sittin' on the floor leaning against the wall. So what's up?" she asked in her enthusiastic way.

Having learned what I needed to know, I cautiously proceeded with what I had to tell her.

"Deb, this is kind of serious news." I paused, said another brief prayer, and went on. "Your dad called from southern California. He went to see another doctor—a different doctor than the one he was going to for his drinking problem. The new doctor is a specialist, and he did a lot of tests on Dad. The results are bad, Debi. The doctor says your dad has AIDS. I'm so sorry to have to tell you this."

Silence followed, broken then by the question, intermingled with sobs, "Mom, is my dad going to die?"

"Yes, sweetheart, he's going to die." My insides ached to tell her such news.

"Mom . . . I feel dizzy . . . I think I . . . "

The phone made a clanging sound. Then nothing. My heart began pounding. I'd lost her!

"Debi! Debi! Can you hear me? Debi, can you answer me? Debi!"

"Heavenly Father, what shall I do?" I prayed. I was panic-stricken. Six hundred and seventy miles separated us. I felt so incredibly far away. I was sure she was having a seizure. How could I get help to her?

"Lord, please help me to think straight," I prayed again.

The line had not disconnected so I tried once more to raise a response from Debi. Nothing. It had always been my habit to keep on talking to Debi when she was in a seizure, so I began to tell her the plan that had come to my muddled brain.

"Debi, I'm going to hang up the phone. Then I'm going to call back to the main switchboard and get you some help. It may take a little while because the main office is a block away. Just as soon as I can get back to you, I will," I said, and quickly hung up the receiver to redial the number.

"Good evening, Multnomah School of the Bible," a pleasant voice said.

"Yes, hello. Please help me. This is Debi's mom. Deb's in the hallway of the girl's dorm. She has received some bad news, and I think she is having a seizure. Please get to her as quickly as you can. I'll stay on the line until you get back to me," I said breathlessly.

"We'll see to her immediately," the voice said.

Endless anxious minutes passed. The distance magnified. At last, the familiar connecting ring to the dorm.

"Hello, Debi's mom?" a young voice inquired. "We're with your daughter. Tell us what to do."

"It's important to allow her to go through the

motions of the seizure," I said. "Don't try to bring her to with smelling salts. Move any object on which she could hurt herself. Please don't be afraid. She usually looses control of her bladder, so please do what you can to save her from embarrassment when she regains consciousness. She'll move about in rigid movements, but she'll be OK. She never chokes, so don't be concerned about her tongue. She automatically turns her head to the side and that seems to protect her from choking. If you can get a wet cloth or paper towel and put it on her face and neck, that will help her to cool down. She's probably sweating by now.

"As she comes to, don't rush her or pick her up. Tell her who you are. And where she is. She needs to be oriented to where she is and who you are. I always tell her over and over, 'It's OK, Debi. It's Mom' until she understands. She'll talk babyish, but she isn't acting. Just talk to her gently. When it's all over she'll be weak. Her muscles will ache. In a few minutes, she's fine and usually hungry. Please let her talk to me as soon as she appears able," I said.

It was a tearful voice, weakened by the trauma of the experience, that came across the line.

"Oh Debi, you poor little pumpkin, are you all right now?" I asked.

"Mama, I want to come home!" she cried.

"I know, sweetie. I wish I could be with you. But God has sent you some very special friends to help you right now. Is there anyone there that you'd feel comfortable confiding in? I think it's important that you have the freedom to talk to someone tonight about your dad. I know it's your tendency to bottle up hard things like this. Is there anyone there, Deb?"

"Yes, I guess so," she responded. "One of the girls here would understand. Here, you can talk to her."

After I had explained the situation, her friend handed the phone back to Debi. I felt assured the girl would come alongside Debi. More than an hour had passed since I placed the phone call. Reluctantly I said my good-byes and thank-yous and hung up the phone. One of the girls had promised to keep a watch over Debi throughout the night. God blessed us with the comfort of His care through the compassion of these girls.

In my usual hang-in-there-through-a-trauma-and-fall-apart-later fashion, I collapsed into a pool of tears. At times like these, I felt so very weak and so very alone. I knew God would take us through, but my feelings had a way of taking over when I became so emotionally drained. Before I finally gave way to sleep, I thanked God again for the people who were watching over Debi. And for the friends who could be depended upon to stand by me as well. The following day I called Jeanie, and we prayed and cried together.

As I thought about Bill's situation, I realized I had no real knowledge about the disease he was facing. Who could I talk to? How could I get any information? How long could Bill expect to live?

About that time KPIX, a local TV station, telecast the movie, *First Frost*, an accurate, informative, and sensitive portrayal of a man afflicted with AIDS. Through this telecast, I became aware of some of the events we would also encounter. It was a strain to watch the movie because it was so true to our lives. It would seem that after so many years of separation, the tendency to identify with Bill or with parallel situations such as the one portrayed in this movie should have subsided. But the unbreakable heart-link that caused me to relate and respond never went away. I felt sorry for the victim. I felt sorry for his family. I felt sorry for the ambulance drivers. And I felt sorry for Debi and for myself. Would the sadness and crying ever end?

It was through the same telecast that I became aware of the AIDS hotline number in San Francisco. The volunteers who answered the phone when I called varied in background. Sometimes when I called, I had the feeling I was talking to a doctor. Other times I would realize the person helping me was a victim of the disease.

Kaiser Hospital offered an all-day seminar that I was able to attend. The man directing the session identified himself as being a medical practitioner and gay. As I continued seeking resources, I was directed to a program designed to uphold the family members of AIDS patients. The woman leading the group stated she was a lesbian. She was also a leader of gay activists. Both in lectures and reading material

I was able to find, the issues of gay rights and safe sex took preeminence.

The hotline number, 800-FOR-AIDS, at the San Francisco AIDS Foundation turned out to be my greatest source of answers to specific questions. I needed to know what to expect of the disease: How does a person die from it? What are the implications of white sores and thirty days of diarrhea? What is the next step of the progression? These are the questions to which I was seeking answers. It was frustrating to learn that Bill's doctor would not respond to my correspondence or to my calls. I thought perhaps they hadn't reached his desk, but a call from Bill told me they had.

"Hi, Sheila. This is Bill." Since the onset of Bill's illness we were calling back and forth between northern and southern California on a semi-regular schedule.

"Hi. How did your doctor visit go today? How are you feeling?" I said.

"Tired. I just don't have any strength. It takes all that I have to get showered and ready to go in to see the doctor. He doesn't tell me much. Just probes and checks. He read me your letter," he said.

"The doctor read you the letter I sent to him?" I asked. It really astonished me that he would do that. "Did he tell you why he won't answer me?" I asked.

"No. He just told me he had received a letter from you and then proceeded to read it. I think it has something to do with doctor-patient confidentiality.

If he answers you, it would be a break in his trust with me, I guess. I don't really know, though," he said.

"Do you know why I wrote to him, Bill? It was for your sake. You've been so scared lately and often confused by alcohol, and I wanted to hear the doctor's perspective," I said. "Do you understand, Bill?"

"Yes. I told him I didn't mind if he responded to you, but I don't think he will. I guess anything in writing could be used against me if you were that kind of a person," Bill said.

"But you know I didn't ask him for the purpose of harming you, Bill. I asked him so I could help you. It's very hard for Debi and me to help you if we're shut out," I said.

"I know. I'll try to keep you updated as best as I can," he said. "I'll call you on Tuesday, right after my next visit."

He was right. The doctor did not respond to me, but Bill followed through in his commitment to call me after his Tuesday visit. The only problem was that several hours at a bar preceding his call altered, exaggerated, and distorted the report.

LIVING IN THE
KNOWLEDGE OF DEATH

Fifteen

The AIDS virus attacks the immune system. Usually the person carrying the virus experiences a number of AIDS-related symptoms occurring at the same time. An individual's ability to resist the various illnesses makes it difficult to predict life expectancy. Bill's most identifiable links to the virus were evidenced through the herpes virus (thrush), chronic diarrhea, and small purple lesions. He became paranoid about catching a cold. He coughed continually. Twice he suffered from pneumonia. Significant dosages of antibiotics brought him through eventually. His strength diminished, and he couldn't work more than half a day when he was at his best.

From all I'd learned of the virus, nothing had been said that would lead me to believe Bill would have the ability to recuperate. But for a time, he did. Periodically through the months following the diagnosis, he appeared to be experiencing very normal health patterns, causing him to believe the doctors had made a mistake in their diagnosis. Then he'd experience a relapse. His strength diminished until he found it an effort to walk across the room. His cough returned. At times I wondered how he could breathe between coughing. He hadn't worked for several months, and he didn't think he could.

Each time he called, I would wonder how much more time he had to live. The lesions on his arms and legs were not the Kaposi's sarcoma I thought them to be. They were ulcer-like sores, about the size of a dime, prone to infection, but still undiagnosed. Bill said cultures had been sent to "City of Hope" for analysis, but so far they remained unidentified sores.

Bill believed the Zovorax he was taking was meant to reduce the lesions. He suffered considerable weight loss, and days went by when he couldn't force himself to eat. Depression became another enemy to tackle. The lesions became infected and reached a dangerous level. Bill was admitted to the hospital.

In about the fourth month, Bill had a high fever. He was delirious and hardly had the strength to whisper a few words at a time. Then he wasn't coherent enough to be understood. Many nights over the next three weeks, we didn't think he'd live through until morning. But he held on. The medicine began to take effect; once again he recuperated, was released from the hospital, and went to live with his sister in nearby Costa Mesa.

Debi and I were doing our best to adjust to the emotional ups and downs related to his suffering. We were beginning to realize we couldn't figure out his life expectancy. The six months that the doctor had expected him to live were almost up, and he was doing better now than a month ago.

The media gave accounts and statistics of the rising problems associated with AIDS, along with the general public's responses and reactions to them. We often found ourselves involved in random conversations in which we felt forced to voice our position. I understood how an attitude of mass hysteria could bring people to conclude that anyone associated with the AIDS virus should be shipped off to some hypothetical island; I just had trouble when these statements were made by Christians. It wasn't a conceivable solution to me to group together hardened drug addicts, flagrant homosexuals, innocent babies, and people whose only crime was their need for a blood transfusion and send them to some infested island. I felt like we needed to be careful not to forget individual dignity—and the power of God. I am convinced this disease is no surprise to God, and, at the very least, we should seek His face for His solution and temper our responses with His compassion.

During the summer, Debi and I proceeded with our plans for a ministry trip with a group from our church to Puerto Rico, Vieques, and St. Kitts in the

West Indies. Our tendency was to stay close to home in the event Bill should take a turn for the worse or even die in our absence. But our stronger inclination was to go on with our plans. There was work for us to do in the service of our Lord, and our lives had known too many postponements. Debi only had a few short months before returning to school, and this is what we felt led to do with the time.

For ten days Debi shared the gospel in an organized team effort with the wonderfully receptive people of St. Kitts. She also was deeply touched by the unswerving faith rooted firmly in the handful of people remaining at the island's leper colony. My responsibilities included photography, shopping for the team's meals, grading correspondence school papers from every island in the West Indies and lower Antilles, and cleaning a rat-infested building. The greatest benefits of this trip, however, were the opportunities to share our story and experiences with Nita, a young woman who wanted to be informed for the sake of helping others, and with the wife of a Christian doctor whose AIDS patients were not willing to be open with him. The ability to help others gave some meaning to our grief, and I knew it was right for us to be there.

The summer quickly drew to a close. We touched down at home, then headed north to take Debi back to school. Since we were so close to my parents, we headed on north to visit them and to see the Vancouver world's fair. It was good to be on "home soil" and to break away from the pressures we had felt for some months now. Recognizing that Mum and Dad were aging, we had in recent years tried to see them at least once a year. Although Debi had not seen her grandfather often when she was young, she adored him as he did her. We had a friendly visit then headed back across the border.

I dropped Debi off at college and continued the journey back alone. Bill felt somewhat threatened by our being so far away and was relieved when I finally responded to the ringing phone.

"Hey, it's good to hear your voice. You were gone a long time," he said. "It was lonely not having anyone to call. I'm glad you're back."

"Is your health doing OK?" I asked. "We thought about you and prayed for you while we were away. Did you receive our postcards?"

"Yes. I didn't know you were in the Caribbean and Miami," he said.

"Well, that's because I told you we were going to South America. I thought Vieques was somewhere near Ecuador. Do you know we had to fly over Cuba? It was a good trip. And we saw some very beautiful sights. It was an experience both Debi and I will cherish as a privilege for a long time to come. All those free-lance art jobs had beneficial returns," I said cheerfully. There was such a fine line between bringing fresh news of life to uplift Bill's spirit and bringing on feelings of jealousy or defeat.

"Bill, does it bother you for me to be telling you about the places we go or the sights we see?" I asked.

"Sometimes. But I'd rather you did, anyway. I'm glad you and Debi are doing these things. I'm really happy for you, Sheila," he said earnestly. "So don't be afraid to talk about it."

"OK, but I'll try to be sensitive, too," I said. "Debi is back in college. It takes me awhile to become accustomed to not having her around the house. I mark the days on the calendar until her next break."

"Sheila, I wonder if I can ask you something? If you don't want to do what I ask, just say so, but I want to ask. OK?"

"Sure, what is it you want to ask?"

"I really want to see you and Debi one more time before I die. Can I come up there and see both of you?" he asked. "I'll understand if you say no. Maybe when Debi has her next school break?"

"Yes, Bill, you're welcome to come if you want to," I responded.

Although I had agreed to his coming, I found myself with a mounting number of apprehensions about the unknowns of the disease. As Bill would not be able to afford a motel, he'd need to stay in our home. I wondered if there were precautions we ought to take for the well-being of each of us. I decided to call the health department, and the lady I spoke with suggested putting a small amount of bleach in the dishwater as well as in the laundry. She also advised us to take every measure of good hygiene—washing our hands often, not using or touching anything that may have been exposed to open sores or to body fluids. With common sense and proper care, we wouldn't endanger ourselves unnecessarily.

Adding to our medical apprehensions were our emotional concerns. I had seen Bill once after dropping Debi off at college, but she hadn't seen him since his initial weight loss. He'd become so terribly thin. We also realized he might back down from coming at the last moment, as he'd done before. It seems to take as much energy to prepare for something that happens as it does for something that never comes to pass. This is a discovery we made each time we prepared ourselves for his death.

Bill arrived, and we searched for a government program that would enable him to stay in the Bay Area. That way he could be near us and also receive qualified care for the combination of alcoholism and AIDS. For ten days I called every agency and referral I could find. Initially we had anticipated having him admitted to San Francisco General Hospital. We were a good way along in the plans when they discovered he was from Orange County and did not have a San Francisco County address. He didn't have the finances to secure an address there, so we had to seek another avenue of help.

We checked into programs that were privately run and available if you had medical insurance plans for them to draw moneys from. And there were alcohol programs, but they required a number of hours per day of work from each participant. Bill had not been able to work for a long time, so he had neither the necessary insurance nor the physical strength to involve himself in a cooperative work program. Every resource seemed to have contingencies he was not able to meet. And so, discouraged and defeated, he went back to southern California.

It was frustrating not to be able to find any help for him. Eventually he secured medical coverage and was put in touch with a support agency that provided him with food, therapy, and the confidence there was someone to call upon if he was unable to care for himself.

Emotionally, Debi and I found Bill's distance from us to be easier to handle in daily living. With the progression of the disease, Bill's tolerance to alcohol and his reactions from overindulgence changed. His tolerance decreased and his reactions accelerated, and I would have found it emotionally troubling to be so close to the situations he placed himself in.

Debi was overwhelmed by the pressures of knowing her dad was dying and being so far away. She decided to complete the fall semester at school then come home to stay. I would have liked her to continue, but I understood how she felt and encouraged her to do what she felt she needed to do. I'd never have asked her to come home for my sake, but it was a comfort to me to have her there.

A NEW GRIEF   *Sixteen*

Just as we were learning to live in the knowledge of Bill's imminent death, we were struck with another blow from a completely different source. Jean called me at the office to ask if I'd please come over to their house directly after work. There was a matter of importance her family wanted to discuss with me. Nervously, I finished out my day's work and left the church office. As I drove the short distance to our pastor's family home, I tried to think what could have made Jean sound so serious.

She greeted me at the door. I could see deep sadness in her face. Her usual bright optimism had been pushed out by the realities now facing her and the rest of her family.

Patiently, I sat down in the front room and waited for her to organize and formulate her words. She sat in the corner of the couch, clutching one of the sofa cushions. Neal entered the room and quietly sat across from us. Jean was so vulnerable, I wanted to do whatever I could to spare her the pain she was experiencing. But, for now, it was best to wait and, when she was ready, to listen.

"Sheila, we wanted you to hear from us what Neal is going to be telling the congregation on Sunday. We didn't want you to hear it there. We wanted to protect you as much as we could ahead of time, so you would be at least a little prepared. We know how much you love us and how you and Debi have become a part of our family," Jean said, then paused. I couldn't even think what she might be about to say, so I braced myself and continued to listen.

"On Sunday night, Neal is going to announce his resignation as senior pastor of Redwood Chapel. I'm sorry, Sheila. We're sorry," she said as she fought to hold back the torrent of emotions these painful words brought her.

"But why? Why is he resigning? It can't be so! Why, Jeanie? I don't understand. Why, Neal? Why do you have to resign?" I asked. Neal and Jean had been on staff at Redwood Chapel for twenty years. In 1980, Neal became senior pastor after Pastor Williams had resigned. They were such a stabilizing force in the church. Yet now they were talking of leaving. I just couldn't understand why.

They explained the issues that had brought about their decision, and I had to admire their sincere concern for the flock. They were seeking to do what was in the best interests of the people entrusted to their care and leadership. The weeks ahead brought them great grief, however, and because I loved them so much and felt so helpless to relieve their pain, I hurt more than I had through any of my experiences of the past.

Not only was Neal my pastor, he was also my boss and our family friend. And Jean was the dearest friend God had ever sent me. And now they were hurting and talking of leaving. I just hated to see them suffer. I agonized, wept, prayed, and wondered why life had to be so unstable and hard.

Day by day I watched the pain they lived through as they severed themselves from the church they truly loved. Day by day Jean suffered. She couldn't eat. She couldn't sleep. She couldn't bear to break the ties. I felt totally helpless. I wanted to stand by her, but everything about me reminded her of Redwood. I wanted to say and do something to take away the pain this family was going through. All our hearts were broken.

Further pieces of the foundation crumbled as various members of the staff and board resigned their positions. Divisions sprang up like unruly weeds. Some members desperately sought to stabilize the church through their tears and pleas before the throne of God. Nonetheless, criticism and distrust filtered through the core of our congregation.

In the midst of the transitions came financial crisis

and our jobs were reduced to a three-quarter time status, adding pressure to each of our lives. Eventually, the church constitution was challenged. Other leaders were challenged. Our personal allegiances were challenged. The church became too painful a place to come to. So I often stayed away.

I watched Jean and Neal pack their belongings including those of their twenty-plus years at the chapel. Moving day came and I helped load the boxes not taken by the moving company. My only consolation was that they had taken a pastorate in a church not too far away. At least we could still spend Thanksgiving and Christmas together.

For a year we lacked a permanent pastor. The other men on the senior staff filled in. At times it seemed like the pressures and dissension weighed so heavily on their backs that you wondered if they would suffer irreparable damage. It occurred to me that forgiveness and submission are learned traits, by the grace of God. It was evident to me that many people within our congregation had not experienced the need to learn these traits and were caught unaware when the need for them arose.

Although we kept in touch as much as we could, Jean was taking on new responsibilities and making new friends. I missed her greatly. She is the one I called when circumstances weighed down on me. She's the one who prayed with me every Saturday for seven years. I was slow to adapt to the change.

At one point, I considered leaving the church and

my job there because of the pain and loneliness that came with conflict and division. I began to look for other opportunities, but did not sense God's leading to a new place. So I withdrew from actively pursuing any change. It was best to be still and wait.

LINGERING PAIN

Seventeen

The average person is not readily equipped to identify the responses of grief, and I was no exception. It wasn't until Debi's fourth accident that I realized that she, too, shared in my preoccupation with Bill's dread disease. First, she backed her car into a parked car. Then she injured herself playing broom hockey, followed by an injury during volleyball. The worst incident, though, was the accident on Mt. Hood.

A group of students was planning a night skiing trip. Debi called me to ask if it was OK if she went along. Borrowing most of the necessary gear, she had narrowed the cost to a mere seven dollars for the night lift. It seemed like it would be a good diversion for her. So, with the predictable cautionary warnings, I encouraged her to go.

And off she went. She jumped off the lift and had barely committed herself to the descent when a sudden fear swept over her. She attempted to stop herself, but her ski caught, came up behind her, and solidly hit her on the back of the head. She fell unconscious. The girls coming up on the lift were startled to see her contorted form lying motionless on the hill beneath them.

Their concern deepened as Debi remained unconscious. They knelt by her side and prayed until the rescue team arrived. Unsure of the nature of her injuries, the rescuers placed her in a metal basket, firmly secured her, then swiftly and capably pulled her in tow down the mountain to the waiting ambulance. Bound for the nearest hospital, the ambulance slipped its way down the ice-laden road, causing the equipment to fly about while the attendant administered oxygen to Debi.

Within a few hours, with X rays and pain killers in hand, Debi was released. Torn ligaments, pulled muscles, and a severe concussion meant she needed to be watched, but at least she could return to the dorm.

God went before us in helping Debi heal and in working through the details of paying back the large portion of the medical bills not covered by our insurance. However, the combination of the prescribed medications, stress, and shock resulted in a drop in Debi's grade level. Even without hindrances, college had not been easy. She was placed on academic probation and returned to school only after special consideration from the dean's office.

It was difficult for both of us to know how much we could safely say to people about Bill's illness. When a family member is dying of a "respectable" ailment, the condolence is kind and full of sympathy. In the case of AIDS, it wasn't so easy to estimate what we would hear. When we'd hardly digested the news ourselves, it especially hurt to hear such statements as, "Well, you know, it's his own fault, and it's God's judgment" or, "He's getting what he deserves." It was hard to believe Christians could so lack in compassion. *If God gave us what we deserved,* I thought to myself, *then premature, terminal illness would be far more prevalent.* I do believe AIDS can be a consequence of action, I just don't believe it's appropriate to state that in a supposed consolation. Love covers, not condemns.

When I heard judgmental opinions, I withdrew to protect us. Sometimes I could sympathize with the lack of understanding. Other times it made me angry and discouraged because I had a higher expectation of Christians than of those who'd never known the love of God.

Some friends wholeheartedly stood by Debi and me, though. They prayed for Bill and inquired about his condition as those whose steps were ordered by unconditional love. Because of these people, Debi and I didn't lose heart on the way.

PAST LOSSES, FUTURE HOPE

Eighteen

As soon as the drug AZT was released for public use by the government, Bill's doctor prescribed it for him. Bill continued to take other medications, including Zovorax for the control of his lesions. Day by day he regained strength and stamina.

Unfortunately, with his new energy, he began to go out and drink again, robbing himself of the full effect of the medications. He didn't seem to have the emotional energy to fight the ever-present battles within or to face his problems when he was sober. Bill's addiction to alcohol had dominated most of his adult life. Habits so ingrained weren't easy to abolish. His drinking was the worst possible thing for him to do at this time in his life. But it numbed the truths now facing him.

The loss of life past was of greater concern to Bill than present losses. What he could have done and didn't, what he could have been and wasn't—these regrets were the source of his greatest heartache. He saw left in his wake time that could never be retrieved, a daughter whom he hardly knew, a God whom he never served. He had bought the lie throughout his life that the present is for self, the future is for God. When the future came, he agonized over his choices. Now he understood the value of integrity and commitment. And he was overwhelmed with remorse.

The phone rang one Saturday morning.

"Hello, Sheila. This is Bill," he said. His voice carried the tone of gentleness that had first drawn me to him. "I was feeling kind of bad, and I just wanted to talk to a friend," he added.

"Hi, Bill. I'm glad you called," I said. "Is there anything I can do to help lighten the load?" Even though I raised the question, I felt terribly inadequate to ease the experiences he faced daily.

"No, not really," he responded. "It just helps to have someone I can call. And to know you don't mind if I'm downhearted. There's a new lesion coming up on my leg and another one on my hand. I'm so scared. I'd rather die than have these ugly things all over me. If they get on my face, I won't go out of my room. I think the doctor is worried about the one on my leg. I have to see him Tuesday."

"We meet for staff prayer on Tuesday morning, so

we'll be sure to pray for you then, Bill. And of course, Debi and I pray for you all the time," I said.

"Thank you. It means so much to know the people at Redwood are praying for me," he said gratefully.

"They are, Bill. And not only the staff, but the youth group and my Bible study group pray constantly as well. Grandma Doty has your name posted in her kitchen, and she prays for you every day. A lot of people stop me throughout the course of the day to ask how you are. So you see, Bill, there are many people who care. Even if they're not sure what they think about the disease, they know how to pray for someone in need," I told him honestly. I knew he would find encouragement especially in the faithful prayers of Neal's mom, whom we all endearingly referred to as Grandma Doty. Through the years, a bond of love had grown between us, and she regularly inquired about and prayed for Bill.

"I know," he said. "And I am grateful. To them and to God. Thank you for caring after all the times I hurt you and Debi. God's love astounds me."

"God wants to ease the way for you, Bill," I said. "Are you sure you're ready to meet Him when the times comes? Are you confident you'll stand before Him cleansed and forgiven?" I asked gently.

On many occasions Bill had called out to God, but for reasons I could not understand, he never had felt the assurance of God's forgiveness and salvation. Because only God can truly know the heart of a man, I was reluctant to conclude whether or not I believed Bill to be saved. The evidence of his life did not uphold his claims, but I did not judge the matter.

Bill's past doubts about his salvation motivated me to probe him whenever I sensed a spiritual sensitivity. Convinced there is no way to the Father except through the redemptive blood of His Son, I often prayed that Bill had accepted that truth and was heaven-bound. Neither Debi nor I could bear the thought of Bill dying with no assurance of where he'd spend eternity.

"Bill, do you know what it is that keeps you from giving up this life-style that has robbed you of everything you've ever cherished?" I asked.

"I know intellectually that God forgives sin. But I've given my whole life to rebelling against Him," he said. "I've resisted His love, His disciplines, and His way of life. Look what I did to you and Debi. How can I ask God to forgive me for that? How can I forgive myself? I wasted every gift He gave to me. I could've served Him so well. And I threw it all away. Now it's too late. How can God forgive me for that? I've violated His purposes and His plans, and it devastates me. My strength is sapped and my life is nearly gone. How can I ever reconcile with God?"

I felt saddened by his frustration. Even though I silently agreed with him about the losses of the past, I knew it was vital to direct his focus away from them and onto the grace of God. So prayerfully I spoke out.

"Bill, the Bible says we've all sinned and come

short of the mark. It also says God loved us when we were still sinners—*before* we got it all together. If Debi and I can forgive you, then you must realize where our ability to forgive finds its source. It's God, Bill. God has put it in our hearts to forgive you.

"You see, Christ didn't come to condemn; He came to redeem. Don't you know, Bill, Jesus died for the very sins you've committed! If you won't accept this forgiveness, then there's nothing more God can do. It means Christ's death on the cross has no value to you.

"Hasn't God held on to you all these years, Bill? Doesn't it amaze you? He keeps drawing you back to Himself. I know it amazes you. You've told me so yourself in the past," I reasoned with him.

"I believe God can forgive me. I don't think I can forgive myself," he repeated. "Then there is the matter of my thought life. I can stop going into the bars, and I can stop doing what I do, but I cannot seem to control my thought life. And that, Sheila, is where the whole gruesome cycle begins and takes its hold on me."

I could hear the desperation in his voice. The number of times he'd lost this private battle to the enemy of his soul were too many to count. True repentance, the kind that includes a renunciation of sin, had eluded Bill. Over and over again, he would claim to have forsaken his sexual sins with their unfulfilled promise to gratify. And over and over again, whether by addiction or by choice, he would submit to the pulls of his inner desires and, beginning with the thoughts, would progress to the deeds that brought about his downfall. The circle would complete itself as he came around to the point of remorse. It was impossible to tell if Bill wanted to change but couldn't do it or if he thought he should change but refused. So around and around he traveled on this road to nowhere—nowhere except death.

We talked a little longer. I did what I could to direct his thinking toward God because I knew God alone was his hope and his means to freedom.

"Well, I'd better hang up," he said. "My phone bill's pretty high already. Thanks for your encouragement. May I call again in about a week or so?"

"Sure," I said. "And please let God love you. Look up Philippians chapter four when you find yourself fighting bad thoughts. Bye for now," I said, placing the receiver down.

Other days, Bill would call after he'd been drinking, and he'd be belligerent and coarse. We made an agreement, therefore, that if he'd had too much to drink, he wouldn't call. And if he made a mistake and did call at such a time, I would ask him to hang up and call me back the next day. This way we avoided arguments that would only tear at the building that was taking place in our relationship.

Sometimes he'd call and ask us to make him some of our favorite chocolate chip cookies and send them down. Other times he'd ask me to print verses on cards for him to hang on his walls as reminders of God's directives. His requests were small, and it was no trouble to fill them. I was glad to bring some kindness into his life.

I could usually identify Bill's mood in the first few minutes of our phone conversations. For several calls now he'd been down and, apparently, drinking often, which caused him to be negative as well. So I put off calling him for a couple of weeks. When I did, I was shocked to find how deep a depression he'd developed. He said he had the kind of anger that makes men kill. I was alarmed by the depth of depression and the intensity of anger he was dealing with. Even though he assured me that he wasn't going to hurt anyone, his words were frightening. His anger grew as he looked back at what he could've been.

He continued to dwell on the past, adding despair upon despair. He refused to be led forward into the present. He denied the power of God. He denied any relationship with God. He wanted to die, but he was afraid to die. The only emotion he allowed himself was great anger. Its demands were acceptable to him. I felt helpless to draw him out of it. I tried to encourage him to seek professional help, but he was too angry to believe anyone could help him.

Bill talked about his resentment toward God for not delivering him years ago. He was mad at his heritage and the incidents of his youth that had led to his choices. He looked at others of apparent success and demanded to know why he had led a life void of accomplishment. He insisted his life amounted to zero—a meaningless nothing. He pressed for an answer to his questions, but in my heart I believed it would benefit him more to express our love.

In the course of our talk, he calmed down to a more pliable frame of mind. Gently and prayerfully, I reminded him that he had fathered a lovely daughter of great worth who loved the Lord and him. I reminisced about the time he'd knelt and heard Debi invite Jesus into her little three-year-old heart. As he talked about the lost years, I cried with him. But I also reminded him of the people who were praying for him.

He was still hostile as he hung up the phone that day. I told the Lord how inadequate I felt and how nervous I was that Bill might bring harm to himself in such a terrible frame of depression. I asked God to protect Bill and to raise him up from the mental pit he'd fallen into.

Bill visited his doctor on a regular basis. Sometimes the doctor was able to alter the medications enough to bring some relief from Bill's cough, fatigue, and general discomfort. Many nights Bill didn't sleep at all, resulting in more anxiety.

One Tuesday afternoon shortly after I had prayed, the doctor met Bill in the waiting room with unusual enthusiasm. The results of the cultures taken from the lesions had come back. For almost a year, doctors had been attempting to conclusively diagnose the lesions so they could treat them. Now, at last, they had the diagnosis and could begin treatment at once for viral tuberculosis.

The Zovorax was discontinued and replaced with a combination of three TB medications that interacted with one another to bring about healing. Bill was filled with new hope. Just as he'd done at the onset of the disease, he again questioned the original diagnosis of AIDS. Looking through a health book, he discovered TB and AIDS had strong similarities. Maybe the doctors had been mistaken, he thought.

It confused me that Bill was able to heal as much as he did for a person who had AIDS. I wondered why the doctors hadn't discovered the TB in any one of the twelve TB tests Bill had had over the past year. I also wondered what the implications were for the people who'd come in contact with him during the time he had TB. And I wondered how TB related to AIDS. Each new phase of the disease seemed to bring a new set of questions.

But this time the questions were short-lived. The doctor still had Bill taking the AZT drug, and Bill's tests had confirmed he had AIDS. We remembered how extremely low his T-cell count had been. Logic and reason brought us back around to the point of reckoning with the facts.

Bill lived much longer than we thought he could. I don't know exactly why. God's timetable, certainly. But beyond that, it's hard to say. His life wasn't shortened by all the abuses—his poor eating and living habits, excessive use of tobacco and alcohol, or irregular consumption of prescription drugs—the way Debi and I had thought. And as the lesions began to heal completely, Bill felt he'd been given yet another extension of time.

Debi and I decided not to try to second-guess the future. We had to deal with each situation as it came to us. Any plans we made with Bill were made with the unspoken understanding they might never come to pass.

CLINGING TO LIFE

Nineteen

Coming into the John Wayne Airport in the L.A. suburbs on December 31, 1987, Debi and I strained to see if Bill was awaiting our arrival. I felt particularly close to Debi as we walked in silence across the tarmac. The difficult encounters with the stresses of our lives continually strengthened the ties between us. We had ventured forth together on unsure ground before. By now we were acutely aware of each other's strengths and weaknesses, both evident and hidden. So we walked in silence, placing no demands on each other, allowing space for private thoughts.

When we had decided to come and see Bill, he was in Hoag Hospital critically ill with pneumocystis carinii pneumonia (PCP). We hadn't thought he'd live. Last-minute flight arrangements were made, but it would be seven days before we could come. By then Bill had once again recuperated and was released to outpatient therapy.

I wondered how we would react to Bill's diminished physical appearance. I wondered how the whole situation would affect Debi. I wondered if we were endangering ourselves coming so close to tuberculosis, pneumonia, and any other viruses his faltering immune system had not been able to fight off. I wondered if our coming would prove to be a positive experience for Bill and if the queasiness in the pit of my stomach would go away. I knew Debi also had her own set of thoughts racing through her mind.

White lines and arrows guided us toward the building where Bill was standing. Bulky woolen sweaters, a jacket and a scarf camouflaged his frailness. His delight at seeing us put a little more color in his face than I'd expected to see. We hugged and nervously chattered for a few minutes. Then, noticing Bill's shakiness, we moved along to find our luggage.

I'd come prepared to rent a car, but Bill insisted he could handle the driving. The hospital where he went for the treatment to clear his lungs was close to the airport, and it was essential that he come every day for at least fourteen days. He asked if we'd go with him. We agreed, and I prayed for Debi, as so many of her previous seizures had taken place when she was at the doctor's or dentist's office or some other medical environment.

As we left the airport parking lot, a more present

concern preoccupied me: Bill's driving! He was doing the best he could, but he'd removed the belt from his power steering and it took every ounce of his strength to bring that old Cadillac around the corner in the same lane in which he'd begun. The Los Angeles traffic whizzed by us on the left and on the right as we sauntered along. We lingered at the green lights and challenged the red. When Bill put the car in reverse at a busy intersection, the look of utter panic on Debi's face could only be matched by that of the man in the Mercedes behind us. Her spontaneous yelp was enough to cause Bill to reconsider and put the gear back into drive.

When we arrived at the hospital, we were so relieved to be safe and sound on solid ground that the impact of being in a hospital waiting room had less effect on Debi than it might have had otherwise. Debi immediately began reading one of her library books while we waited the thirty minutes that it took for Bill's treatment.

In a very few days, Bill would exceed the two-year maximum life expectancy given to people with full-blown AIDS. The very costly and extensive lung treatment, along with the newly approved AZT drug and a number of other prescribed medications with long names (clofazimine, ehionamide, and rifampin), contributed to Bill's ability to hang on to life.

It surprised me to note how well the sores on his forearm had healed. I'd had the impression AIDS patients couldn't heal. And without the amount of antibiotics and other medications that had been poured through his ailing body, he probably wouldn't have. The sores on his legs, however, were still present and needed constant cleansing and care to prevent them from becoming gangrenous. Some days Bill would be diligent in changing the bandages. Other days, he just didn't feel like he had the strength or the will to do it.

Although Bill still clung to life, it appeared as though his days of "doing" were now spent. The strength he had was barely sufficient to carry him through the essentials of daily living. I felt that all the unfinished tasks of his past or his future would remain unfinished. His mind was foggy, his bones were tired, and he needed to lie down to keep from coughing.

We left the hospital and precariously found our way to our motel. In the morning Bill arrived so we could accompany him to the hospital again. Because it was New Year's Day, we had to go to the main hospital rather than the nearby clinic. Again, I wondered how it would be for Debi.

Christmas wreaths and garlands provided a point of focus as we slowly walked past Nuclear Medicine and Radiation Therapy to the Pulmonary Therapy and Rehabilitation Unit. Upholstered chairs with oak accents sat neatly in a row behind three oak and glass topped tables. One corner of the small waiting room was softened by tiny, twinkling lights on a carefully decorated life-like Christmas tree, while the other corner held a suspended television set tuned to channel 5. Two small therapy rooms, a washroom, a nurse's station, and an oversized fish tank containing a variety of orange and white carp took up the remaining wall space. As we studied our surroundings, we found the details of the room to be a pleasant distraction to our anxiety.

Our eyes were drawn again to the television set as the familiar voice of Bob Eubanks described, with practiced flourish, the spectacular floats of the 99th Annual Pasadena Rose Bowl Parade. We sat and waited until Bill's name was called. A glance in Debi's direction seemed to indicate she was handling the situation. The therapist arrived, and I was impressed with the quality and courtesy of care extended by the hospital staff each time we came.

Within an hour of his treatment, Bill would cough so continuously that I would actually fear for his life until it subsided. By the second day of our visit, I also observed a rising level of anger.

"Bill," I asked, "can you explain the anger you're feeling? I know you are glad we're here, yet I can feel the anger, and I wondered if it would be a help to you to talk about it to us."

"I just want to be able to do more for you and Debi," he said. "And I can't even stop coughing. I haven't got any strength, and it makes me mad."

"Bill, we didn't come here to be entertained, remember? We came to do things for you, not for you to be doing things for us," I reminded him. "The fact that you're out of the hospital and able to get around this much is far more than we expected when we made our decision to come."

"I know," he said, "but I'm so very weary of never feeling well. It makes me angry inside, and it embarrasses me."

It was hard for Debi and me to know how to encourage Bill. The last time we'd visited, he spoke of death and wanted to talk about issues related to his memorial service. But this time, he spoke as though he expected to get better and return to work. We neither encouraged nor discouraged his thinking. We discovered it wasn't wise to get into heavy discussions dealing in logic because he either would not or could not respond well. Sometimes he was motivated by his stubborn will and then, other times, his overwhelming fear. Sometimes it seemed like his brain no longer had the capacity to handle everyday situations, and we would realize our company and support were more important than anything we had to say.

Our flight home wasn't scheduled until Sunday evening at nine. We knew Bill could not withstand the cooler night air or stay up that late. So about three-thirty in the afternoon, I asked him to take us to the airport. We had our books to read and felt better knowing we hadn't overtaxed Bill.

Bill put forty-five minutes' worth of coins in the parking meter, and we came into the airport and waited in silence. I knew he felt badly about his condition. It was difficult to know what to say. We all knew we would probably never see one another again. As the time neared for the meter to expire, Bill stood up and hugged Debi and me. He felt so utterly frail to the touch. My heart ached as I watched him walk slowly to the door, turn to wave a last good-bye, then vanish into the crowd. Tears spilled involuntarily. We each struggled with our emotions. I prayed God would watch over Bill in his lonely existence.

HARD PRESSED, BUT NOT CRUSHED

Twenty

As the years slip by, I think of the strange mix of my life. Fondly I recall the childhood years—summers at the cove by cool inlet waters; secondhand bikes and countless hours of freedom; Saturday morning and countless lists of chores. Then came the teen years— art school and dates and traveling adventures across the South Pacific to the "Land Down Under." There was a lightheartedness in me then and a naive conviction that a little hard work combined with a lot of determination could open the door to any dream. I thank God for that outlook. It created picturesque memories that I could walk back to when the road I later found myself on grew barren and colorless.

Even though the losses throughout the years have been many, and even though my dreams died in the face of painful reality, I don't perceive the past as wasted. When I remember to look at the eternal perspective, I see a different picture, a different set of values. I see God's enduring love directed toward Bill, patiently providing opportunities for him to experience His mercy firsthand. And I see God's enabling strength directed toward Debi and toward me, providing us with the grace to believe, heal, care, and forgive.

From time to time, I regret that my life had so much disappointing pain. Occasionally I find myself longing to be pampered and cared for by a loving husband. And more than once, I have wished I could be at home baking the bread instead of out "winning" it.

Nevertheless, I know that God has a plan for me. I believe Jeremiah 29:11, which says: "'For I know the plans I have for you,' declares the Lord, 'plans to prosper you and not to harm you, plans to give you hope and a future.'" I'm thankful I came upon this verse shortly after Bill left when it felt so much like there was no future for me at all.

Knowing God has a plan has caused me to look in His direction and desire to serve His purposes.

Knowing God has a plan for me enabled me to return to the Fremont Health Department with my receipt in hand to discover the results of my HTLV 2 test, and to know if I was to live or to die.

I walked up the same grey stairs as I had ten days earlier. This time a friend accompanied me instead of tears. Even though I knew it was all in God's hands, I appreciated the presence of a reassuring companion. Jean would have come with me, but she and Neal had an important reunion to attend in Chicago all week. I knew their prayers were with me as we followed the mute arrows and entered the waiting room.

"Claudia, why don't you sit here while I let them know my number?" I asked my friend.

"Are you OK?" she asked.

"Yes, I'll be fine," I said, praying that God would help me.

The receptionist took my receipt. "Thank you. Please be seated. The nurse will call for you," she said.

Claudia and I quietly sat and waited. I reflected on verses of Scripture tucked away in my heart for moments such as these: "I will never leave you or forsake you" (Josh. 1:5); "We are hard pressed on every side, but not crushed; perplexed, but not in despair; persecuted, but not abandoned; struck down, but not destroyed.... Therefore we do not lose heart. Though outwardly we are wasting away, yet inwardly we are being renewed day by day. For our light and momentary troubles are achieving for us an eternal glory that far outweighs them all" (2 Cor. 4:8-9, 16-17); "God is our refuge and strength, an ever-present help in trouble" (Ps. 46:1). I thought about how much I love God and how thankful I am for His salvation. I admitted to Him that I didn't really want to die. I was not afraid to die, but I was afraid of all the ailments associated with AIDS that preceded death.

And I was afraid of the lonely alienation that many AIDS patients suffer.

The nurse appeared in the doorway, signaling me to follow her. I searched for the answer in her face, but her expression remained unreadable. We entered the same little cube-sized room as before and sat across from one another. The nurse checked over the papers in her hand, then glanced up with a gentle smile and said, "I am happy to inform you your tests have come back negative. You are not carrying the AIDS virus."

"Thank you, Lord," I whispered, "Thank you for sparing me."

The nurse walked me out to the front office. Claudia didn't need to ask the result. The expression on my face said enough!

As we drove back toward the valley, I realized afresh how great is the mercy of God. I knew now why God had permitted me to secure a divorce. In 1980 I hadn't even heard of AIDS, and could not, therefore, have protected myself from it. I was confirmed in the importance of following God's edicts because only He knows the end from the beginning. Then I thought of Bill's whole situation and realized why it is so important not to give ourselves to the pulls of the things around us. I felt that the early choices of his life were summed up in the verse, "There is a way that seems right to a man, but in the end it leads to death" (Prov. 14:12).

ON THE TWELFTH DAY OF JUNE

Twenty-One

Incredibly, Bill rallied into his third year with AIDS with little observable change from the year before. His excessive drinking, however, resulted in the loss of housing, rapidly reducing him to the ranks of the homeless.

When he told me he was living out of his car, I was inclined toward pity. I wanted to come to his rescue, but I had to remember my previous efforts to relocate him to our area had failed. I also had to remember there was little I could do to regulate his drinking or its consequences. Agencies far better equipped had opened their doors to help and then, because of his drunken abuses, were pushed to the point of closing them again.

Debi and I also had to think about the potential

hazard of exposing ourselves to his variable infectious ailments, which now included tuberculosis. It would have been unwise to remove him from the Orange County support and health care services, which were providing ample moneys to keep him off the streets if he would only use the money as it was intended. So we resisted the emotional impulse to bring him back into our home and remained burdened for the next few weeks until we received word that he was either in some kind of shelter or rooming house again.

We resumed our telephone conversations with an increased regularity. I began to wonder if the perpetual slur and other irregular behaviors mimicking drunkenness were actually indicators of progressive, permanent brain damage. Common words and familiar phrases were an effort for him to recall. A gripping fear brought about strange behavior in Bill as the real merged with the imagined in his fevered mind. Delusive images of swarms of bees hovering outside his door kept him a prisoner in his room. Sometimes our words calmed him; sometimes they did not.

Amid his paranoia, Bill became frightened enough by the way he was feeling and the persistent headaches he was having to go to the emergency room of the local hospital. A life-threatening swelling between the skull and the brain prompted doctors to schedule immediate surgery. Shaken, Bill called to forewarn us of this latest discovery and then signed the consent, cognizant of the risk of paralysis, blindness, or death. We spoke to him, knowing this could be our last conversation, and found great comfort in Bill's calm readiness to meet the Lord face-to-face. Bill was prepped and on his way to the operating room when the doctors took another look at his chart and postponed the surgery until his white cell count could be raised enough to provide at least a minimal chance for survival.

Four days later he was rescheduled and somewhere in the early hours of the morning the surgery was completed. Once again, to our utter amazement, Bill pulled through yet another threat to his life without negative side effects. By the following day, we were able to talk with him while a nurse held the phone. He spoke slowly and clearly, without the slur or the confusion of the month past. Within two weeks he was released to a hospice care home in Tustin. There he received full nursing care and assistance with the small tasks of daily living. He gained a little more strength each day, and soon he was able to get around with the help of the nurses and a wheelchair. Now that the paranoia was gone, Bill welcomed the chance to get outside again. Unfortunately, to the sheer horror of the accompanying nurse, he would stubbornly insist on driving his car himself, until his car was ultimately taken away from him.

Confined again, Bill began to spend much of his day just lying in bed. We talked on the phone often, and the hospice care workers spent long periods of time keeping him company and encouraging him deep into the lonely night. But his loss of weight that brought him down to ninety-one pounds and the continuing headaches were taking their toll on him. He had been told he could not survive another surgery if it became necessary and if the presence of AIDS became more and more apparent.

We often thought of going to see Bill, but the same pride that ruled his youth brought him to a state of panic at the thought of Debi and me seeing him in this advanced stage. In addition, Bill was sure he did not have the strength to withstand the emotional highs and lows of our coming and then leaving again. So together we agreed that our calls and our prayers would benefit him more in the long run than our visit.

As awkward as it felt, we set aside time on his good days to discuss what to do at the time of his death. During our visit two years before, Bill had told us who was to receive his belongings and expressed his wishes regarding the content of his memorial service to be held at Redwood Chapel.

He told us the county and the AIDS Services Foundation (ASF) would take care of his burial because of his indigence. He did not wish to be placed on life support systems and, unless it would bring comfort to his sister, he saw no reason for us to come until we were ready to pick up the few mementos of drawings, paintings, poems, and household items he had left for Debi. He was honored that Neal Doty and Joe Linn would officiate a service in his memory, and he assured us all was in order. He had even begun to long for death and was at last ready to go before a holy God, assured of His forgiveness and grace.

One afternoon Debi called Bill and was shocked as the nurse told her that her father was in pain throughout his whole body. He had also lost the strength to speak. The nurse then offered to hold the phone to his ear and encouraged Debi to talk to him even though he could not respond. Pulling her emotions in check, Debi sweetly expressed her love and offered complete forgiveness for any harm done in the past that Bill might still be burdened by. She softly conveyed her sorrow at his latest reversal and encompassing pain. The nurse then related his efforts to smile in response to her words of love.

Within the hour, Bill was taken by ambulance to the hospital where an attempt was made to insert a catheter through his chest to send a steady flow of morphine to block the pain. The efforts were unsuccessful, and he was taken back to the hospice where further attempts to penetrate his collapsing veins finally brought a measure of relief. As he was heavily sedated and under twenty-four-hour nursing care, we had little opportunity to communicate with him. More than we'd done in over the past three years, we were inclined to put our lives on hold.

We found ourselves hesitating when it came to

making plans that would take us away from home. But the coupling of everyday stress with the heavy wait of impending death made it all the more vital to break away on occasion. After some encouragement, Debi agreed to a few days of vacation with the Iveys in Sacramento. As June approached, with my first month-long holiday, I still resisted making plans. It was only after a long, persuasive talk with Debi that I finally conceded to pack a suitcase, dig out my camera gear, and head north in the quiet solitude of my car.

I set out alone on a Sunday morning, driving toward the Oregon and Washington coast and ultimately across the Canadian border. My brother David flew west from Calgary to Vancouver where we met and spent time photographing the parks and coves of our youth. After a day of touring we returned to our parents' home, barbecued the evening meal and were in the process of cleaning up our few dishes when the phone rang. David answered, and a man's voice asked for me.

"Hello, Sheila. This is your neighbor, Taso. Debi asked me to call you," he said in a subdued tone. "I have some bad news to give to you."

"Has Bill died?" I asked, knowing the answer before I posed the question.

"Yes. I'm sorry. He died this evening," he responded.

"Yes, I'm sorry, too, Tas. Is Debi OK?" I asked with mounting concern.

"She's OK. She's crying, but she's OK. She just wanted me to call because it's hard for her to put it into words," he said showing a maturity beyond his twenty years.

"Thanks, Taso. How about you, are you OK?" I asked.

"Yeh, I'm OK. Sorta. It's just hard to think Bill is dead because I remember him from when he lived here. It's hard to think he is dead."

"That's how I feel too. Death is a hard thing to face," I said with a heavy heart. "May I talk with Debi? Does she want to talk?"

"Sure, I'll get her for you," he said.

"Will you look after her for me, Taso?" I asked.

"Yes, you can be sure I will."

"Will you stay there at the house as long as she needs you? I really don't want her to be alone at all," I said.

"Yes. Don't worry, I'll take care of her," he said as he handed over the phone.

Debi and I spoke briefly. She and Taso had grown up together and were as close as brother and sister. She assured me she would be all right. We both knew Jean and Neal would have taken her into their home at a moment's notice, but Debi felt more comfortable staying in her own surroundings. She was confident that being with her friends would be as important to her as being with my brother was to me. We had learned a long time ago that we process things differently. Debi would want to be silent. I would want to talk. Now, instead of two grieving people trying to appease and uphold one another, we were both being upheld by others who cared about us and could withstand our unrestricted leaning.

Walking away from the phone, I felt a deep sense of loss. The news of Bill's death carried a heavy finality. For the next hour or so David sympathetically listened while I talked about the early years of my life with Bill. He neither hurried nor interrupted me, but patiently allowed me to express my emotions through words rather than tears. He gave me the freedom to say what I needed to say. Drained, I decided to wait till morning to call Debi again before making any decisions. We said good night, and I went to my room and quietly wept for the man I had loved.

And so it was, on the twelfth day of June 1989, at 6:15 P.M., Bill slipped from the confines of his pain-ridden, eighty-seven-pound body into the presence of the Lord. His grief, at last, was over; his struggles were finally done.

The next morning I spoke again with Debi, and although I had offered to come home at once or to fly her up to Canada, she preferred to stay with our original plan. I decided to comply with her desire for me to continue on up through the Canadian Rockies to visit my brother's family in Calgary, Alberta. Taso and his friends were standing with Debi—listening, making phone calls, and watching over her. As word reached our friends and church family, Debi was further supported by their calls, cards, and invitations to their homes. It was hard for me to think of Debi arranging her father's memorial service, but in a way it helped her comprehend the reality of his death and begin the vital process of closure.

My thoughts then began to dwell on Bill's presence in heaven, and although I cannot begin to conceive what heaven must be like, I did find great comfort in the thought that Bill was there. David and I continued with our plans to join his family. After our visit, I drove back alone down through the Crow's Nest Pass, along the Columbia River, west toward the Oregon coast, and into California. As I got closer to home, I could feel myself responding sadly to the reality of Bill's death, and suddenly, for no reason, I was overwhelmed with tears. Now it was time for Debi and me to comfort one another.

VICTORY PARADE

Twenty-Two

Turning the key in the chapel door, I shuddered at the eeriness of the darkened, silent room I was about to enter. Immediately I felt the conflict between past memories of a thriving place of worship and present realities of a room now seldom used. I smelled musty air as I walked across the small narthex and peered through the glass partition. Bill's service would take place here in a very few hours.

Bill hadn't attended Redwood Chapel for a number of years, and the smaller chapel building that was familiar to him had been replaced by a 2,100-capacity worship center. But Bill had remembered the chapel as his church home, so this is where he wanted his memorial service to be. As we planned the service some two years earlier, we had wondered if the pain it produced was worth the effort. Now, as I stood in the empty chapel, it was a great comfort to know rather than guess what songs and words would be pleasing to Bill.

As I stood contemplating what was soon to take place, it occurred to me to ask Debi to come to the chapel now, too. We could experience how it felt to walk in and sit in the row of pews designated for the family, and we could talk a little about our feelings and the service before it actually took place. Debi had never attended a memorial service, so I wanted to reduce her possible apprehension of the unknowns. We were also planning to display a number of Bill's pencil drawings and oil paintings on easels as well as photographs taken of Debi and him over the years. Setting them up would occupy our hands and prepare our minds for what would take place that evening.

When Debi arrived, we stood for a while in the narthex then walked together through the subdued light to the front of the church. Beautiful arrangements of flowers softened the podium and platform areas, and our hearts were touched by the sweet thoughtfulness of those who'd sent them. Debi and I reverently sat in our designated pew.

We then decided to ask Jean, Shannon, Sean, and Grandma Doty to join us in the family row because, regretfully, nobody from our family was expected to come, and except for a niece, no one from Bill's family would be coming either. Neal had read us the contents of his notes a few days ago, so we were aware of what he was planning to say. Once Debi and I felt we'd had enough time alone in the church we went out to the narthex, finished setting up Bill's works of art, and walked away feeling better prepared.

We returned at six o'clock. This time when we walked through the chapel door, the lights were on and Jean was waiting to greet us with a hug, Neal and Joe Linn, a friend and musician, were rehearsing "Day by Day," and the eeriness was gone. I set a special little leather book that Bill had given Debi on the podium in the entry for guests to sign. Debi was comfortably talking with Shannon and Sean, so I proceeded to watch for Bill's niece whom I hadn't seen since she was small.

The small folder I'd prepared to be given out stated, at Debi's insistence, Bill's given name—William Hamilton Eby—followed by his assumed name—William Ronald Bowerman. We were done with secrets. Inside the folder was a poem written by Bill, set to music and later sung by Sean Doty in the service. It was dedicated to Debi and expressed Bill's confidence in God's acceptance of him.

As friends began arriving, we were given hugs of compassion and thoughtful words of support. Joe Linn gently, masterfully played the piano while we were being seated, and then Neal began:

"Friends, this service is being held in loving memory of William Hamilton Eby, known to most of us as Bill Bowerman. Bill attended Redwood Chapel, was a member, and worked on the staff as a custodian for some time. His wife, Sheila, and daughter, Debi, are still very much a part of this church, where Sheila is a staff member.

"I spent many hours with Bill talking about the Lord. We studied the Word of God together, and he was often in our home. And some have wondered out loud why this memorial service would be held in Bill's memory by the wife and daughter he deserted and from whom he was divorced. The answer is that we love Bill and we love the Lord. It's because of God's grace and mercy that we are here. Bill's story, and that of his family, is a story of God at work in lives."

Neal's articulate manner of speaking was mixed with the gentle concern of a caring pastor. As he looked in Debi's direction with a kindness in his eyes, he conveyed a message of reassurance. And I slipped my arm in hers as she reached down for the box of Kleenex.

"At times of sorrow and loss, we Christians go to God's Word for comfort and hope. Paul's letters were a source of hope for Bill in his life. Paul wrote to the Romans in chapter five, 'Therefore, since we have been justified through faith, we have peace with God through our Lord Jesus Christ, through whom we have gained access by faith into this grace in which we now stand. And we rejoice in the hope of the glory of God' [Rom. 5:1-2]. The concept of grace, God's grace—His unmerited favor made available to us just because He wants to—is beautiful.

"And that's what Bill came to understand: God's grace, God's goodness to him, the reason for joy for a Christian. As Romans 5 says, 'You see, at just the right time, when we were still powerless, Christ died for the ungodly. Very rarely will anyone die for a righteous man, though for a good man someone might possibly dare to die. But God demonstrates His own love for us in this: While we were yet sinners, Christ died for us' [Rom. 5:6-8].

"And John 3:16, a verse loved by many was also one of Bill's favorites: 'For God so loved the world that he gave his one and only Son, that whoever believes in him shall not perish but have eternal life.'

"When Debi was little and the family had learned of the work of Christ, they would say to each other, 'Well, whoever goes first, save a place in line!' They knew death was no longer something to fear. A few months ago when Debi and Sheila visited Bill, he said, 'Well, it looks like I'll be going first—I'll save you that place in line.' Bill was counting on the words of God through the apostle Paul when he wrote, 'For we know that when this tent we live in now is taken down—when we die and leave these bodies—we will have wonderful new bodies in heaven, homes that will be ours forevermore, made for us by God himself, and not by human hands [2 Cor. 5:1]. Everyone dies, but all who are related to Christ will rise again!

"Bill was passionate about everything in life. Right

or wrong, he did everything in a big way. And Bill was passionate about his pursuit of God. The picture of walking in close and unblemished fellowship with the holy God enthralled him.

"Bill deeply desired to know God in that way, but he struggled with patterns of life that were established long before he met Christ. Addictions to alcohol and sex often overcame him. He died a few weeks ago from AIDS as a direct result of that other life that haunted him. Bill believed that God could set him free from his addictions and forgive his sin, yet he still knew awful cycles of victory and defeat.

"But today, Bill is with the Lord—set completely free! At last he's completely clean, done with the struggle with sin that so often weighed him down.

"In Bill's last few days, God was finally victorious in his life. And when the wonder and beauty of that victory over sin moved him, Bill wrote this poem which Sean has set to music. The words are there in your folder."

As Sean approached the microphone and positioned his guitar, I turned to Debi and asked if she was OK. I wondered if she would make it through the service without fainting or going into a seizure. With an effort, she smiled. She seemed all right. Sean capably, softly began to sing "Victory Parade."

> There was a Victory Parade
> In heaven today (and)
> The Lord of all the armies

was there in His place
Of honor and praise.

(And) the battle's all won,
His praises to be sung,
But He called to me and said,
"Come share My victory
And share My joy,
For in Me you have overcome
And My Victory is yours."

Debi clasped my hand and breathed a tremored sigh as Neal resumed his place at the pulpit.

"Bill was a sickly child, and perhaps that had something to do with the lonely struggles he faced all his life. He became a man who had to be the best at whatever he did. The problem was that from his expectations and perspective, he could never do it well enough. He could never satisfy himself.

"I'm glad to see that out in the narthex are some of the pictures Bill did. And it's amazing there are still some of these we can enjoy because I have seen a number of things Bill did that I thought were tremendous that he destroyed because they did not meet his expectations."

That is so true, I thought, instantly recalling the paintings and drawings not found among Bill's belongings. How many times I had watched him paint over a completed oil with layer upon layer with dark, heavy strokes of the brush until the original work was lost.

"Bill was a perfectionist daunted by his own imperfections. And that desperate search for acceptance for a good feeling about himself led him to search sometimes for good feelings in wrong places.

"It took him years and a lingering illness to come to a place where he took God at His words, 'Not by works of righteousness which we have done, but according to His mercy He saved us' [Titus 3:5]. It took a long time for Bill to really believe that God would receive him as he was. Bill desperately wanted to be worthy of God's grace. He wanted to clean himself up first and then present himself to God. At the same time he felt he never could or never would be worthy of God's grace. It was a battle of the years—the yearning to be acceptable to God battling the sense that he could never merit that acceptance.

"But the day did come—and not long ago—when Bill realized and experienced God's grace and forgiveness—and deliverance. It was then that the cycles of victory and defeat were brought to an end. In the ultimate victory of God's grace over man's sin, it was God's victory. A victory of life over death. Of wholeness over illness. Of light over darkness. Of salvation over sin. Of forgiveness over faults and failures. And it was a victory of acceptance, at last, over loneliness and alienation."

Neal paused and then began to sing the song, "Ninety-and-Nine." The sheep who stood off in a place of danger until the Lord went to get him represented a perfect word picture of Bill. I thought about all the times Debi and I were safe and Bill was off in the dangers of the night. And I thought about the morning he was scheduled for brain surgery when the Lord went to get him. I couldn't hold back the tears any longer. Neal conveyed a look of compassion, then continued.

"God triumphed in Bill's life at last. And Bill shares in that victory and triumph today in God's presence. He will never suffer trial again. He'll never suffer temptation or pain. Or fear. Or frustration, anger, sorrow, or despair. He will never again be enslaved by the passions he embraced with self-hatred and loathing. The storm is past. The confusion is over."

At this point, my heart filled with thankfulness and relief as I envisioned Bill experiencing these new freedoms. Through all the years of Bill's anger and refusal to commit, God had waited, ready and capable of delivering him from the life-style he had chosen. And now, because at last Bill had submitted himself to God, he was free. Neal's next words affirmed that.

"These are Bill's sentiments: 'I stand before God not guilty only because of His mercy and not on my own merit, for I am as guilty as they come. First God's mercy and then His love. Because without His mercy, I would have never experienced His love.'

"Bill explained his struggles with the Christian life this way, 'I thought: I'll take this time for me and later [time] for God. But it doesn't work at all. It's a delusion of the mind. You cannot say, Let me take what I want now and God comes later. It is totally untrue!'

"John Oxenham wrote these words so expressive of Bill's sense of God's grace at the last:

In that I have so greatly failed Thee,
Lord have grace.
And in Thy outer courts
Deny me not a place.
So little of fair works
For Thee have I to show.
So much of what I might have done,
I did not do.

Yet, Thou hast seen in me at times
The will for good
Although so oft I did not do
All that I would,
Thou knowest me through and through.
And yet, Thou canst forgive.
Only in the hope of Thy redeeming grace
I live!

"Probably only two things keep people from God's grace. One is to believe, as Bill did for so long, that you're too bad, that you're not good enough for God's grace—and perhaps there are some in that category here today. May I assure you that God's grace is open; it's available to *you*. The other belief that might keep some from coming to God for His grace is that you're not bad enough, that you're too good to need His grace. The Bible says, 'For all have sinned, and come short of the glory of God. . . . For the wages of sin is death; but the gift of God is eternal life through Jesus Christ our Lord' [Rom. 3:23; 6:23].

"I'm sure that if Bill were here today, he would want me to extend the invitation that he himself received that you might experience forgiveness of sin and right standing with God. A 'not guilty' status before God is available to you because of God's favor extended at the cross of Jesus Christ, who died in your place that you might live forever. What a wonderful truth!

"Our God, as we have come to this time of remembering the life of one who is very special to many of us—a dear friend, family member, a great talent, a man who at his best moments shared generously, and loved—we thank You for Bill. For that which was good about him was You at work. And we thank You for Your grace and for Bill's discovery of Your provision for sin in the Lord Jesus Christ. Thank You that Bill discovered the truth of the good news that Christ died for our sins; He was wounded for our transgressions; He was bruised for our iniquities. Thank You for what Jesus did. Thank You for what You did in the life of Bill Bowerman. We give You praise for eternal life in Jesus' name. Amen."

Joe again softly played the piano, and Neal escorted Debi and me from the family row back to the narthex. As the people came out, we could see that the message of this man of God had touched hearts with the reality of God's grace. And in this hour of recognizing the power of God's incredible mercy, I felt deep within me the fading of the inequities of the years. Our prayers had been answered. And as I look at the broader view of God's eternal purposes, I feel our losses are few and the struggle was worth it.

A NEW CHAPTER *Twenty-Three*

With doors and windows standing open, the August breeze deftly moved from room to room, carrying the pleasant aroma of country fried chicken and hot apple dessert. Debi's imminent arrival, already delayed two days by a broken tow bar, kept me from fully concentrating on the dinner I was preparing. I soon expected to hear the throbbing vibrations of an approaching truck.

It still amazed me that Debi was driving from Portland to Castro Valley alone, in a large rented truck, with all her belongings inside and with her car in tow. Although her youthful determination combined with our prayers led me to believe she could do it, I wasn't going to be completely at ease until I actually heard her coming up the street.

She finally arrived—exhausted, completely out of

fuel, hungry, and safe! We ate and we talked until four in the morning. I had fully supported Debi's decision to return to Portland shortly after Bill's death, but now, fourteen months later, I was so very glad to have her back home.

On the day Debi drove away, Taso promised to watch out for me and had faithfully kept his word. Denise and Brian, the young couple next door, along with Claudia and the Doty family had made my time of transition easier with their phone calls, visits, and invitations to dinner. Good friends were there for me through problems as trivial as a weekend with no one to talk to or problems as traumatic as the 1989 San Francisco earthquake when freeways and buildings collapsed around us. But the empty feeling that came after Bill's death and Debi's departure persisted. For her sake I tried to conceal my loneliness, but Debi had perceived it and ultimately decided she was coming back home.

Even though it wrenched our hearts to be apart, progress was taking place for both of us during the time Debi was up north. She shared a comfortable townhouse with a college friend and took on the responsibilities of independent living. She began attending church and joined the gym to keep up on her sports. She worked a full schedule, and as time permitted, she coached volleyball to the handicapped.

By God's great provision, I completed my writing of this book and mailed my proposals to prospective publishers. When the phone call came from Tyndale House, I was thrilled and humbled to realize my manuscript had been accepted. In the weeks that followed, through the help of a friend, I attended my first writer's conference at Mount Hermon. There I met with Ken Petersen, an editor from Tyndale House, and dared to perceive myself as a soon-to-be-published author!

I put every dollar I had in the bank toward the purchase of a Mac computer for the books not yet written. I changed my place of worship to Fairmede Alliance Church where Neal and Jean had accepted a pastorate. And I started teaching a ladies' class there.

It is exciting to realize how pain-free and normal my life is becoming. I think my tendency toward insecurity and loneliness will remain a part of me for a while to come, yet every time I need the confidence to make a new friend or to speak of God's great goodness to me, He gives it to me. Hurtful memories of past disappointments are fading, and the only purpose in looking back comes from the desire to tell others how God helped us—and how He will help them. As God enables me to use our negative experiences for the good of others, I find encouragement and optimistically wonder what the future holds.

Debi's life is also changing. She has fallen in love with a young Christian man named Denny. Her glowing countenance and perpetual smile reinforce her claim to love him, and at the time of writing, plans are underway for their wedding. As we are preparing and rejoicing together, we look forward to God's blessings on our future.

EPILOGUE

Having come through the deep waters of a marriage where every dream is dashed by the deeds of an abusive mate and having discovered there the protective care of a loving God, I now stand on the sure footing of the distant shore with a compelling desire to reach back to offer help and hope to those still being pulled down at the hand of another.

When a person of integrity is bound in marriage to a person of deceit year after painful year, hope dies. The insurmountable weight of shame and alienation drags the spirit down and opens the door for confusion and compromise. The unrelenting pain circles endlessly, wearing at the stability of the reasoning powers of the mind. Self-respect vanishes as the lie is lived out.

After years of pleading, questions are thrown into

the lonely, empty space of night: Will the pain ever go away? Will my life always be plagued with humiliation and with defeat? Is it too much to ask to be loved? Will my mind hold together, or will I be robbed of my sanity along with everything else? Does God—or anyone—care? What difference does it make how I respond after so much unfaithfulness and abuse? Why should I forgive over and over again? How much can I stand? What happened to the sanguine dreams of my youth? What's the use of trying to be good when my whole life is so terribly bad?

Now, some twenty years later, the questions have all been asked and answered and proven. When peace of mind and self-esteem are regained and when the cutting pain finally subsides, there is no doubt as to the care and protection of God. There is victory and spiritual growth. And when one parent's ability to forgive is reproduced in a child, all experience freedom and compassion.

In addition to my primary goal of offering hope to the one in need, I had a secondary purpose in writing this book: to urge the Christian community into awareness and to express the need for compassion. The issues of today's news are not distant statistics. Innocent people are being crushed by the rebellious deeds of family members. Innocent victims sit in the divorce courts. Innocent children live in the shadow of sexual abuse. Drunken brawls take place in Christian homes. The cunning of a master deceiver is too devious for the naive, and the blameless are left incriminated and broken. Children are asked to cope with adultery, homosexuality, and AIDS.

Will our children know that the Christian community recognizes these facts and cares? Will God, who judges all things well, be honored by our love? This is the challenge we each must face.